Home Lawn Management in South Carolina

Extension Circular 687
Revised June 2009

by Bert McCarty, Ph.D., Turf Specialist, Clemson University,
and Robert F. Polomski, Extension Consumer Horticulturist, Clemson University

Clemson University Public Service Publishing
Clemson University
Clemson, SC
2009

Published by Clemson University Public Service Publishing
Copyright © 2009 Clemson University

Printed in the United States.

Find Clemson University Public Service Publishing on the World Wide Web at http://www.clemson.edu/psapublishing

Library of Congress Control Number: 2009930137

ISBN 978-0-9798777-3-5

Revised June 2009

Table of Contents

Home Lawn Management In South Carolina

Bert McCarty, Ph.D., and Robert F. Polomski

Introduction

Turfgrass adds beauty and value to any property and is one of the most versatile and functional plants in the landscape. Turfgrass enhances the environment in many ways which are particularly important in urban areas. Turf is one of the most effective plant covers to reduce soil erosion and surface runoff while recharging ground water, which results in more efficient use of rainfall. A turf area reduces heat by as much as 30 °F below that of a concrete or asphalt area and as much as 14 °F below that of bare soil. The cooling effect of the average lawn is equal to over 8 tons of air conditioning, which is twice that of the average home central air conditioning unit. Turf also absorbs dust and other air pollutants, and produces oxygen. Turf also provides the best surface for outdoor activities.

Identification

Although turfgrasses have many characteristics useful for identification, flowering or seeding parts are generally needed for absolute identification because other plant parts can be affected by environmental factors. Table 1 provides some general characteristics useful for identifying common turfgrasses and grassy weeds. Figure 1 illustrates these structures. **Stolons** are above-ground stems and **rhizomes** are below-ground stems. Both are capable of growing a new plant and allow a grass to creep or grow laterally allowing the plant to cover areas damaged or thinned by insects and disease. **Texture** refers to leaf width. The **ligule** is the structure which clasps the stem at the junction of the blade and sheath. The **bud leaf** is the arrangement of an emerging leaf or leaves in the budshoot. In general, they may be classified as rolled or folded. For example, the new shoots of tall fescue are rolled. The new shoots of centipedegrass are folded.

Selection

Perhaps the most important factor in establishing and maintaining an attractive and problem-free lawn is to choose a turfgrass that is adapted to your region and to your particular landscape. The turfgrass should also have the qualities you desire. Trying to establish a turfgrass species in an area where it's unsuited requires special management techniques to produce a quality lawn. Since a lawn is intended to be a permanent planting, selecting the right turfgrass is an important first step. Selection should be based on a few of the following elements: region of adaptation, tolerance to local environmental conditions, the level of turf quality you desire, the level of maintenance you are willing to provide, and potential uses for the lawn.

The right type of grass—one that suits your needs and is adapted to local conditions—will always give better results. Grasses vary in the type of climate they prefer, the amount of water and nutrients they need, their resistance to pests, their tolerance for shade and salt, and the degree of wear they can withstand.

If you are establishing a new lawn or renovating an old one, do some research to identify the best kind of grass for your lawn. If you are working with an established lawn that fails to thrive despite proper care, you may have selected the wrong type of turfgrass for your growing conditions. Consider replanting with a different kind of grass that is adapted to your area.

This publication is adapted from *The South Carolina Master Gardener Training Manual*. 2008. Bob Polomski, ed. Clemson Circular 678, Clemson University Public Service Publishing, Clemson, SC. Portions were excerpted and adapted from *Southern Lawns; Best Management Practices for the Selection, Establishment, and Maintenance of Southern Lawngrasses*. 2003. Bert McCarty, ed. Clemson Extension Circular 707, Clemson University Public Service Publishing, Clemson, SC.

Figure 1

Illustration of the various parts of a grass plant. The primary leaf structures used to identify grasses are the ligule, auricle, collar, and sheath.

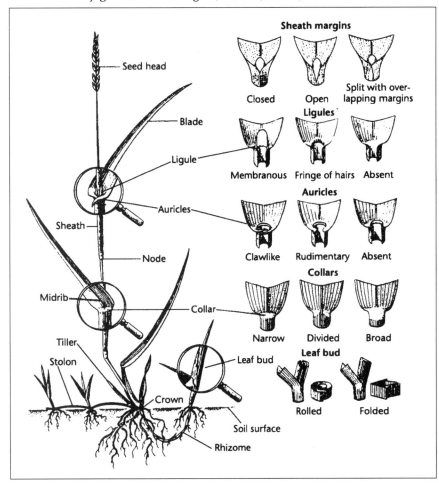

Region of Adaptation

Turfgrasses are placed into one of four climatic categories based on their adaptation. These four climatic categories are the cool humid, warm humid, cool arid, and warm arid regions. Turfgrasses that are adapted to the cool humid and irrigated cool arid climatic regions are the **bluegrasses, fescues,** and **ryegrasses**. They are called **cool-season turfgrasses** (Table 2). **Warm-season turfgrasses,** which are adapted to the warm humid and irrigated warm arid regions, are **bahiagrass, bermudagrass, carpetgrass, centipedegrass, St. Augustinegrass, seashore paspalum,** and **zoysiagrass**.

South Carolina has a warm humid region with a transition to cool humid in the Piedmont. Cool-season turfgrasses are better suited to the Piedmont and Mountains. In the transition zone throughout the Piedmont, both cool- and warm-season grasses can be grown. Warm-season grasses are well-suited to the Sandhills and the Coastal Plain. Tall fescue, a heat-tolerant cool-season turfgrass, could be culti-

vated in the Sandhills, but it would require a high level of management.

Tolerance to Environmental Stresses

When selecting a turfgrass for your lawn, select one that tolerates various local environmental stresses. These stresses include seasonal temperature extremes, moisture availability, possibility of salt problems, amount of available sun or shade, and the amount of traffic the turf will have to tolerate.

Turfgrass Quality and Maintenance

The quality of lawn you desire is also important in the selection process. Decide if you want your lawn to be a showplace, average-looking, or just a functional living cover that controls soil erosion. An attractive, average-looking lawn will require less time and effort than a superior-looking, weed-free lawn.

Lawn quality is directly related to maintenance. Moreover, most turfgrasses have an optimum level of maintenance that includes fertilizing, mowing, watering, and pest management. In general, a low level maintenance approach entails little fertilizing, mowing as needed, and seldom, if ever, watering. A medium level of maintenance requires more frequent fertilizing, mowing weekly, and watering as needed. A high maintenance level lawn requires frequent fertilizing, twice-per-week mowing, yearly dethatching, regular watering during the growing season, and controlling pests.

Turfgrass Use

The final consideration in turfgrass selection should be how the lawn will be used. Certain species of turfgrass are more adapted to heavy traffic, while other species are more adapted to lighter use. Planting species that are slow-growing or are marginally adapted to the climate of the area will thin out from heavy use and may need to be reestablished every year.

Table 1

Identifying characteristics of turfgrasses and grassy weeds.

Common Name	Scientific Name	Stolons	Rhizomes	Color	Texture[1]	Leaf Ligule[2]	Leaf Bud[3]	Other Characteristics
Bahiagrass	*Paspalum notatum*	YES	YES	Med-dark	C	SM	R-F	Two to three spiked seedhead.
Bermudagrass	*Cynodon dactylon*	YES	YES	Med, light-dark	C-F	H	F	Tillers grow at 30-60° angle; some hairs on leaf surface; long stolons.
Bluegrass, Annual	*Poa annua*	NO	NO	Light	F	LM	F	Boat shaped leaf tip, dual veins in middle; smooth leaf.
Bluegrass, Kentucky	*Poa pratensis*	NO	YES	Med. dark	M	SM	F	Boat shaped leaf tip; dual veins in middle; smooth leaf.
Carpetgrass	*Axonopus affinis*	YES	NO	Light	C	SH	F	Two to five spiked seedhead. "Wavy" leaf margins.
Centipedegrass	*Eremochloa ophiuroides*	YES	NO	Light	C	SM	F	Single spike seedhead blades, hairy along edges; has natural yellow-green color.
Fescue, Red	*Festuca rubra*	NO	FEW	Medium	F	SM	F	Leaf very narrow, needlelike and usually folded.
Fescue, Tall	*Festuca arundinacea*	NO	FEW	Medium	C	SM	R	Leaf margin rough to touch; red stem base; veins prominent; auricles small, hairy.
Orchardgrass	*Dactylis glomerata*	NO	NO	N/A	C	LM	F	Stem very flat; blue-green color; seed contaminant in tall fescue.
Ryegrass, Annual	*Lolium multiflorum*	NO	NO	Light	C	SM	R	Underleaf shiny; red stem base; veins prominent.
Ryegrass, Perennial	*Lolium perenne*	NO	NO	Med-dark	M	SM	F	Underleaf shiny; red stem base; veins prominent; clawlike auricles.
St. Augustinegrass	*Stenotaphrum secundatum*	YES	NO	Med-dark	C	SH	F	Boat-shaped leaf tip, single spike seedhead.
Zoysiagrass	*Zoysia* spp.	YES	YES	Med-dark	C-F	H	R	Stiff to the touch; sheaths compressed; tuft of hairs at collar; hairy on leaf surface.

[1]C=coarse; F=fine; M=medium   [2]M=membraneous; H=hairy; S=short; L=long   [3]R=rolled; F=folded

Cool-Season Turfgrasses

Cool-season turfgrasses grow best during the cooler months of the year. The ideal temperature for growth is 60 to 75 °F. They may go dormant or be injured during the hot months of summer. These grasses are better adapted to the Piedmont and Mountains of South Carolina (Table 2). An advantage to planting cool-season grasses is that all of the species adapted to the state can be planted from seed, which is the most economical way of establishing or renovating a lawn. These grasses will remain green throughout the year, with the most attractive color during fall, winter, and spring.

A disadvantage of cool-season grasses is their high susceptibility to diseases and crabgrass invasion during the warm, humid summer months. This can result in complete loss if the lawn is neglected or managed improperly. In areas where cool-season turfgrasses are limited due to environmental adaptation, they will thin and may need to be reseeded annually during the fall months.

The most popular species for home lawns is tall fescue. Chewings fescue, red fescue, and Kentucky bluegrass are adapted only to the mountainous regions of the state. Red fescue is well-suited for shady areas. Bentgrass is also adapted to this area, but is used predominantly on golf course putting greens. The ryegrasses are suitable only for temporary covers in areas where a permanent turf is to be planted and for winter overseeding of dormant warm-season lawns.

Tall Fescue (*Festuca arundinacea*)

Tall fescue is perhaps the most popular grass used in the Mountain and upper Piedmont regions of South Carolina. Tall fescue is a perennial, bunch-type grass that is considered a good utility turfgrass. It establishes quickly from seed and grows well in full sun to partial shade. It is adapted to a wide range of soil conditions, preferring a fertile, moist, fine-textured soil that is high in organic matter. Soils exhibiting a pH range of 5.5 to 6.5 are best suited for tall fescue, but this grass will tolerate

Table 2

General comparisons of the major cool-season turfgrasses for South Carolina lawns.

	Chewings Fescue	Kentucky Bluegrass	Perennial Ryegrass	Red Fescue	Tall Fescue
Area Best Adapted	Mountains	Mountains/Upper Piedmont	Mountains	Mountains/ Piedmont	Mountains/ Piedmont
Growth Habit	Bunch	Rhizomes	Bunch	Bunch	Bunch
Establishment Rate	Very slow	Slow	Very fast	Medium	Medium
Mowing Height	$1\frac{1}{2}$ to $2\frac{1}{2}$	$1\frac{1}{2}$ to $2\frac{1}{2}$	$1\frac{1}{2}$ to $2\frac{1}{2}$	$1\frac{1}{2}$ to $2\frac{1}{2}$	$2\frac{1}{2}$ to $3\frac{1}{2}$
Mowing Frequency	Medium	Medium	Medium-High	Medium	High
Days to first mowing after seeding	14 to 21	30 to 35	7 to 14	12 to 17	14 to 21
Disease Tendency	Medium	Medium	Medium	Medium	Low
Drought Tolerance	Excellent	Good	Good	Very good	Excellent
Heat Tolerance	Fair	Fair	Poor to Fair	Fair	Good
Salt Tolerance	Good	Poor	Good	Good	Good
Shade Tolerance	Excellent	Poor to Fair	Fair	Excellent	Good
Thatch Tendency	Medium	Medium	Low	Medium	Low
Wear Tolerance	Fair	Good	Poor	Good	Good

a pH range of 4.7 to 8.5. It can tolerate wet soil conditions as well as periods of submersion, and is often used in drainage ways.

Tall fescue grows rapidly during the spring and fall months, requiring frequent mowing. It shows good heat and drought tolerance for a cool-season turfgrass. However, it may thin out if irrigation is unavailable and if rainfall is lacking. Tall fescue will remain green during most of the summer and winter, but grows little during periods of extreme heat or cold. A drawback to planting tall fescue is that it tends to thin-out and become "clumpy" if not properly managed or if it is planted in an area to which it is not well-adapted. Reseeding will be required in the fall to maintain an adequate stand of grass.

Kentucky-31 is the old, common variety of tall fescue. Most of the new cultivars referred to as "turf-type" tall fescues have slightly narrower leaves, darker green color, slower vertical growth rates, greater density, and better shade tolerance than K-31. Some varieties of turf-type tall fescue have better disease resistance and drought tolerance than others. In general, most properly managed turf-type tall fescues will produce a better-looking lawn than K-31.

Fine Fescues (Festuca species)

Fine fescue is a collective name for several fine-leaved species of grasses in the genus *Festuca*. Native to the cool, forested European Alps, fine fescues have delicate wiry leaves that are usually less than $^1/_{50}$-inch wide and have a clumpy, bristlelike appearance. Red Fescue (*Festuca rubra*) and spreading fescue (*F. pratensis*) have slow spreading rhizomes, while chewings fescue (*F. rubra* ssp. *commutata*), sheep fescue (*F. ovina*), and hard fescue (*F. longifolia*) have a bunch-type growth habit.

Hard fescue has a deep green color, whereas sheep fescue is bluish-green. Red or creeping red fescue is adapted to shady locations in cool, moist Mountain areas. Chewings, hard, and sheep fescues tolerate full sun or partial shade. They are often planted in shaded, low traffic areas. If left unmowed, their leaves and seedheads provide a low maintenance, natural look.

As a group the fine fescues are noted for shade tolerance, winter hardiness, and adaptability to infertile, dry soils. They do not tolerate wet, poorly drained soils very well, but are adapted to dry, shady conditions and low maintenance situations. They do not tolerate extensive traffic or heat, and do not persist below the upper Piedmont region (<1,000 ft. elevation) except as clumps in shaded areas.

Fine fescues are rarely used alone, but are often mixed with other cool-season grasses such as Kentucky bluegrass and perennial ryegrass. They are also used in blends for winter overseeding of warm-season turfgrasses.

Red fescue tolerates shady conditions better than any of the other cool-season grasses. It is often used in mixtures with Kentucky bluegrass. Red fescue tends to prevail in the shade, while bluegrass dominates the stand in full sun.

Kentucky Bluegrass (Poa pratensis)

Kentucky bluegrass is adapted to the upper Piedmont and Mountain regions (elevation > 900 ft.) of South Carolina. Soils that are moist, well-drained, and fertile, with a pH range of 6 to 7, are best suited to Kentucky bluegrass. It does best in full sun, but certain varieties tolerate partial shade. These shade-tolerant varieties are often mixed with red fescue for shady areas.

During dry periods in the summer, Kentucky bluegrass may turn brown and go dormant. However, Kentucky bluegrass is capable of surviving an extended drought and can initiate new growth from underground stems or rhizomes when moisture conditions are favorable. To maintain a green Kentucky bluegrass lawn in South Carolina in the summer, irrigation will be needed during dry spells.

When planted on a well-adapted site and properly managed, Kentucky bluegrass will provide a quality turf, although a high level of maintenance will be needed. If managed poorly, thatch can become a serious problem, particularly with vigorous-growing varieties maintained at a high level of management.

Annual Ryegrass (Lolium multiflorum)

Annual ryegrass is not a permanent lawn grass. As its name suggests, it is an annual species that dies out the following spring and summer after being planted in the fall. It is used to establish a quick cover during the winter to control erosion on sites that cannot be planted with a permanent turfgrass due to cold temperatures.

Annual ryegrass is also used by itself or in a mixture with other cool-season grasses as an over-seeded grass for green color during the winter on dormant, warm-seeded lawns. When used alone, annual ryegrass will provide a marginal overseeding cover, but it does not handle environmental stresses well. It often dies out before the winter is over.

Perennial Ryegrass (Lolium perenne)

Perennial ryegrass is similar to annual ryegrass in many ways, but usually lives a little longer when the right conditions exist—usually an extra two to four weeks in the spring or early summer. As with annual ryegrass, perennial rye is used to cover bare areas in the fall and winter and to provide winter color to dormant, warm-season lawns.

Perennial ryegrass is superior to annual ryegrass due to its increased heat and disease resistance. Susceptibility to certain diseases in the summer still makes them unreliable as permanent lawns. Many fine-textured varieties are available that have more disease resistance and possess better mowing qualities. Often, they may survive for several years in cooler environments, particularly in the absence of competition from other grasses. Still, their use should be limited to overseeding warm-season lawns.

Warm-Season Turfgrasses

Warm-season turfgrasses grow best during the warmer months of spring, summer, and fall. The ideal growing temperature is 80 to 95 °F. Certain warm-season grasses will turn off-color during the driest periods of summer. All warm-season turfgrasses will become dormant during the winter, but will resume growth with the warming temperatures of spring.

Seven warm-season turfgrasses are commonly grown in South Carolina: bahiagrass, bermudagrass, carpetgrass, centipedegrass, seashore paspalum, St. Augustinegrass, and zoysiagrass (Table 3). Bahiagrass, bermudagrass, carpetgrass, centipedegrass, and zoysiagrass will grow from the Coast to the Piedmont. Seashore paspalum and St. Augustinegrass are well-suited for Coastal areas.

Bahiagrass (Paspalum notatum)

Common bahiagrass was introduced from Brazil in 1914 and was used as a pasture grass on the poor sandy soils of the southeastern U.S. The ability of bahiagrass to persist on infertile, dry soils and to resist most pests, especially nematodes, made it an increasingly popular lawn grass where function is more important than appearance.

Generally, bahiagrass will not provide as fine a lawn as the other warm-season turfgrasses described in this section. It is suitable for out-of-the-way areas where a low-maintenance vegetative cover is needed.

Bahiagrass can be inexpensively grown from seed. Once established, it develops an extensive root system that makes it highly drought-resistant.

Bahiagrass has a relatively open growth habit and produces tall, unsightly seedheads from May through October. The prolific seedheads and the tough leaves and stems make it difficult to mow. For the best appearance, bahiagrass should be cut with a heavy-duty rotary mower.

Bahiagrass is poorly adapted to alkaline or high pH soils, and will not thrive in areas subject to salt spray. Compared to other lawn grasses, bahia has fewer pest problems, although mole crickets can cause severe damage.

Four varieties of bahiagrass seed or sod are sold for lawns: **Common, Argentine, Paraguay,** and **Pensacola.**

- **Common** bahiagrass is the least attractive type because of its light green color, coarse texture, and prostrate, open-type growth habit. Also, it has poor cold tolerance and is not recommended for use in home lawns.
- **Argentine** is the best variety for lawns. It has wider leaves than Pensacola, but longer and narrower leaves than Common. It forms a dense sod, has good color and cold-hardiness, responds well to fertilization, and produces few seedheads. Argentine is least susceptible to dollar spot disease.
- **Paraguay** is also known as "Texas bahia." It has short, narrow, very hairy leaves that look grayish in color. Paraguay has low cold tolerance and is very susceptible to dollar spot disease.
- **Pensacola** bahiagrass was selected from plantings found in Pensacola, FL, in 1935, and it has become the most widely grown bahiagrass variety. Pensacola is used extensively along roadsides in the southern U.S. due to its deep, fibrous root system and readily available seed. Although Pensacola produces seedheads with abandon, its long, narrow, blue-green leaves have made it the second best lawn grass behind Argentine.

Seashore paspalum (Paspalum vaginatum)

This relative of bahiagrass is also known as sand knotgrass, siltgrass, and saltwater couch. Seashore

Table 3

Adaptations and characteristics of warm-season grasses.

	Bahiagrass	Bermudagrass	Carpetgrass	Centipede	Seashore paspalum	St. Augustine	Zoysia
Area Best Adapted	Statewide excluding Mountains	Statewide	Sandhills to Coastal Plain	Statewide excluding Mountains	Coastal Plain	Coastal Plain	Statewide
Establishment Method	Seed or sod	Seed[a], sod, plugs, or sprigs	Seed or sprigs	Seed, sod, plugs, or sprigs,	Sod, plugs, or sprigs,	Seed, sod, plugs, or sprigs	Seed, sod, plugs, or sprigs
Maintenance Level	Low	High	Low	Low	Medium	Medium	Medium-High
Mowing Height (inches)	3 to 4	$3/4$ to $1 1/2$	1 to 2	1 to 2	1 to $1 1/2$	$2 1/2$[b] to 4	$3/4$ to 2
Mowing Frequency	High	Very high	Low	Low	Medium	Medium	Low to Medium
Mower Preference	Rotary	Reel	Rotary	Rotary	Rotary	Rotary	Reel
Cold Tolerance	Fair	Fair to Good	Poor	Fair	Very poor	Poor	Fair to Good
Disease Tendency	Low	Low	Low	Low	Medium	Medium	Medium
Drought Tolerance	Excellent	Excellent	Very poor	Fair	Fair-Good	Good	Excellent
Nematode Tolerance	Very good	Poor to Fair	Poor	Poor	Poor to Fair	Fair to Good	Poor
Salt Tolerance	Very Poor	Excellent	Poor	Poor	Excellent	Good	Good to Excellent
Shade Tolerance	Poor	Very Poor	Fair	Fair	Poor to Fair	Good (cultivar dependent)	Fair
Thatch Tendency	Low	High	Low	Medium	Medium	Medium	High
Wear Tolerance	Good	Excellent	Poor	Poor	Good	Fair	Excellent

[a]Common bermudagrass varieties only.   [b]Dwarf St. Augustinegrass varieties only.

paspalum can be found growing along the coastal regions of North Carolina through Florida and west to Texas. Often growing in brackish water, it has the highest salt tolerance of any turfgrass. Seashore paspalum has dark blue-green leaves and spreads by rhizomes and above-ground stems called stolons. Several types are available that either resemble coarse-leaved common bermudgrasses or fine-leaved hybrid bermudagrasses. It produces a fairly dense turf when mowed regularly at $1\frac{1}{2}$ inches or less.

Seashore paspalum does not tolerate prolonged freezing conditions as well as bermudagrass. Thus, it appears that currently available varieties are limited to coastal areas. Seashore paspalum tolerates more shade than bermudagrass, but less shade than other turfgrasses.

In addition to older varieties such as **Excaliber** (formerly Adalayd) and **Futurf**, newer selections have been released in the U.S. They include **AP-10, FWY-1, Salam, Sea Isle I** (for golf course tees and fairways), and **Sea Isle 2000** (for golf greens), which are vegetatively propagated by sprigging, plugging, or sodding. Other worldwide varieties include **Boardwalk, Durban CC, Enviro-green, Enviro-turf, Ecoturf, Mauna Kea, Saltene, Salpas, Seagreen, Seaway,** and **Tropic Shore**.

Bermudagrass (Cynodon species)

Bermudagrass is a long-lived turfgrass that is adapted throughout the state. It thrives in a wide variety of growing conditions and soil types, and tolerates a wide soil pH. Bermudagrass is also quite salt-tolerant, which makes it a good choice for coastal regions where salt sprays and flooding occur.

Bermudagrass produces an aggressive, dark green, dense lawn which is adapted to the soil and climatic conditions in South Carolina. It has excellent wear and drought tolerance, which makes it ideal for home lawns, parks, golf courses, and athletic fields. Bermudagrass establishes rapidly and competes well against weeds.

Bermudagrass' aggressive nature can be troublesome. It will spread by both above- and below-ground runners which can become difficult to control in groundcovers, flower beds, and walkways. However, bermudagrass will not tolerate shade; it will gradually thin out and disappear under trees or building overhangs.

Bermudagrass requires a high level of management to attain a showcase quality lawn. Because of its rapid growth rate, mowing practices should include a reel-type mower. Rotary mowers will work fine as long as the blades are sharp.

Due to its nature to grow rapidly, thatch buildup can become a problem with bermudagrass. Common bermudagrass tends to accumulate less thatch than hybrid bermudagrass.

Bermudagrasses have very few serious pest problems, but are subject to attack from sting-nematodes when grown in sandy soils. Nematode damage leads to shallow-rooted plants that do not respond to water and fertilizer, resulting in thin, weak areas invaded by weeds. If you suspect nematodes, submit a soil sample for analysis.

Common or hybrid bermudagrass varieties can be used in home lawns. Common bermudagrass (*Cynodon dactylon*) is a rather spindly grass which is considered a weed ("wiregrass") by many people, but it can become a quality lawn grass with proper management.

In recent years, improved types of common bermudagrass have been released. Many of these "improved" grasses look similar to hybrid bermudagrass varieties; however, they have the advantage of being planted by seed. Also, these newer types are able to cope with environmental conditions better than the older common bermudagrass. Several improved varieties of common bermudagrasses include **Celebration, Cheyenne, Mirage, Sahara, Yuma,** and others.

Hybrid bermudagrasses (*Cynodon* x *transvaalensis*) are superior to common bermuda. They produce no viable seed and must be sprigged, plugged, or sodded. Compared to common, hybrid bermudagrasses have more disease resistance, greater density, better weed resistance, fewer seedheads, finer and softer texture, and the most desirable color. The hybrids also demand the highest degree of maintenance for the best appearance of any of the warm-season grasses, such as frequent close mowing, regular fertilizing, edging, and dethatching.

The most popular hybrid bermudagrass-variety is **Tifway**.
- **Tifway (Tifton 419)** bermudagrass has a dark green color, medium-fine leaf texture and shoot density, moderately low growth habit, and a rapid growth and establishment rate. Among the hybrid bermudagrasses, this is the choice for home lawns.

Carpetgrass (Axonopus affinis)

Carpetgrass is a creeping warm-season grass native to the West Indies that closely resembles centipedegrass. Carpetgrass is not widely used as a lawn grass in South Carolina, but is sometimes used on soils that are too infertile or too poorly drained for bermudagrass. It is especially adapted to soils that stay wet for most of the year.

A carpetgrass lawn usually has a rough or ragged appearance because of seed stems that are hard to mow. It grows well in sun or partial shade if the soil is moist, but tolerates less shade than St. Augustinegrass and centipedegrass.

Carpetgrass is very shallow-rooted, and has poor drought tolerance and cold hardiness. It turns brown with the first cold spell and slowly greens up in the spring.

Centipedegrass (Eremochloa ophiuroides)

Centipedegrass was introduced into the U.S. from southeastern Asia. It is a slow-growing turfgrass adapted from the Coastal Plain to the Sandhills. It has a natural yellow-green color (described by some as "Granny Smith-green") and spreads by centipedelike stolons—hence the common name. It is adapted for use as a low maintenance, general purpose turf. Centipede requires less fertilizer or mowing than other warm-season grasses. Since it only produces surface runners, centipedegrass can be easily controlled around flower beds and along walkways. It is the ideal grass for anyone wanting a fairly attractive lawn that needs little care.

Common centipede can be established from either seeds, sprigs, plugs, or sod. Since it is slow-growing, it takes longer than bermuda and St. Augustine to completely cover newly planted areas.

Centipedegrass is more shade-tolerant than bermudagrass, but cannot tolerate shade as well as St. Augustine and zoysiagrass.

Centipedegrass has a few liabilities. It is susceptible to winterkill during extremely cold winters. Also, it does not tolerate traffic, soil compaction, high-phosphorus soils, low-potassium soils, or high pH soils.

Centipedegrass is also susceptible to several diseases. Brown patch and dollar spot can cause extensive damage when conditions are right for the disease to flourish. It is also very susceptible to ground pearls and plant parasitic nematodes. These two soil-inhabiting pests can be quite destructive on centipedegrass.

A disorder called "centipedegrass decline" usually occurs in the spring when parts of the lawn fail to come out of dormancy. Sometimes parts of the lawn start to greenup and grow, but then die in late spring and summer. Several factors cause centipedegrass decline, including a high soil pH, high amounts of nitrogen and phosphorus the previous year, heavy thatch buildup, nematodes, and diseases that make the grass susceptible to injury.

Most of the centipedegrass that is available in the marketplace is of the common variety. It an be established by seed and through vegetative means. Because the seed is rather expensive, it is usually planted by sodding or plugging.

Improved varieties of centipedegrass are available, such as **Centennial**, **Oaklawn**, **TennTurf**, and **TifBlair**. These improved varieties have better cold tolerance than common; however, they can only be planted by plugs or sod—not by seed.

St. Augustinegrass (Stenotaphrum secundatum)

St. Augustinegrass or "Charleston grass" is adapted to the warm, humid southern regions of the U.S. and grows well along the South Carolina coast. St. Augustinegrass has large flat stems and broad coarse leaves. It has an attractive blue-green color and forms a deep, fairly dense turf. St. Augustinegrass spreads by runners or stolons, which can be easily controlled around borders. It prefers well-drained, fertile soils. For an acceptable quality lawn, St. Augustinegrass requires irrigation and moderate level of fertility during the growing season.

St. Augustinegrass has good salt tolerance and will handle shade better than other warm-season turfgrasses. Establishment is quick and easy from sod.

St. Augustinegrass has several characteristics that may limit its use in certain situations. The coarse leaf texture may be objectionable to some people. During drought conditions it will not remain green without supplemental irrigation. It has poor wear tolerance and can be damaged by cold temperatures. Excessive thatch can become a problem under high fertility and excessive irrigation. The major pest problem associated with St. Augustinegrass is the chinch bug; however, chinch bug resistant cultivars are available. St. Augustine Decline Virus (SADV) is a major disease problem in some parts of the U.S., but it has not been a problem in South Carolina. Other diseases include gray leaf spot and brown patch.

Here are just a few of the many cultivars of St. Augustinegrass that are available for home lawns:

- **Common** and **Roselawn** are pasture-types. Avoid planting these cultivars if appearance is important.
- **Bitterblue** is an improved variety selected in the 1930s for its finer, denser texture and darker blue-green color than Common. It has improved cold tolerance and good shade tolerance, but is not resistant to chinch bugs or gray leaf spot disease. Bitterblue can produce a good lawn under proper management practices and pest control.
- **Floralawn** is similar to Floratam in shade tolerance, coarse leaf texture, and sensitivity to cold temperatures. It is resistant to chinch bugs, sod webworms, brown patch, and SADV. Floralawn can be grown in full sun to moderate shade under low to moderate fertility.
- **Floratine** is an improved selection from Bitterblue with similar characteristics. It has a finer texture and lower growth habit which allows closer mowing than common St. Augus-tinegrass. Floratine is not resistant to chinch bugs, but tolerates light to moderate shade.
- **Floratam** is an improved type of St. Augustinegrass with a very coarse texture and resistance to chinch bug and SADV. It grows vigorously in open sunny areas. Floratam has relatively poor cold and shade tolerance. Spring greenup is also slow.
- **Jade** and **Delmar** are darker green, have better cold tolerance, and improved shade tolerance compared to Seville. Jade has a finer leaf blade and better shade tolerance than Delmar. Delmar has increased cold tolerance; therefore, it can be grown in cooler regions. Due to their semidwarf growth habit, Jade and Delmar should be mowed between $1^1/_2$ to $2^1/_2$ inches. Both are susceptible to chinch bugs, sod webworms, and brown patch disease. Jade and Delmar grow slowly, so they require a longer period of time to establish from plugs or to recover from damage compared to other cultivars.
- **Palmetto** has a semidwarf growth habit, good color, moderate shade tolerance, and relatively good cold tolerance.
- **Raleigh** is a cold-hardy cultivar that has a medium-green color and a coarse texture. It is susceptible to chinch bugs, but is probably the most cold hardy of the St. Augustinegrass cultivars. This cultivar is the one most commonly planted in the Sandhills and Piedmont because of its cold tolerance. During the peak heat of summer, Raleigh may slow in growth and not spread as well as it would during the cooler seasons of spring or fall. Supplemental applications of iron may be needed to reduce yellowing from iron deficiency. Raleigh is ideally suited for heavy clay soils with a medium to low soil pH.
- **Seville** is a semidwarf variety with a dark-green color and low growth habit. It has a finer texture than Floratam. Seville will grow well in shade and makes an excellent turf in full sun. It is susceptible to chinch bugs and sod webworm, resistant to SADV, and is cold sensitive. Due to its compact growth habit, Seville is prone to thatch buildups and shallow rooting.

Zoysiagrass (*Zoysia* species)

Zoysiagrass (*Zoysia* spp.) is adapted to a wide range of soils and has good tolerance to cold temperatures, shade, and salt spray. Zoysiagrass is one of the most cold-tolerant of the warm-season turfgrasses. It performs well in full sun or partial shade, but will thin out in dense shade.

Zoysiagrass forms a low, slow-growing, very dense lawn that resists weed invasions. The slow growth habit is an advantage because it can be mowed less frequently than other grasses and is easier to keep out of flower beds than bermudagrass. However, zoysiagrass is tougher to mow than other warm-season turfgrasses.

The improved cultivars of zoysiagrass must be planted by vegetative means and are extremely slow to establish. Two growing seasons may be needed to cover a lawn with zoysiagrass when planted by plugs or sprigs.

All zoysiagrasses form a heavy thatch layer, especially when mowed high or infrequently or when fertilized heavily. Thatch needs to be removed periodically by dethatching. Care should be taken when dethatching zoysiagrass because of its slow growth rate.

Zoysiagrass recovers slowly from injury, grows poorly on compacted soils, has a high fertility requirement, and requires frequent watering during the summer months. It looks best when mowed with a reel-type of mower, although an attractive appearance can be achieved using a rotary mower with sharp blades.

There are several species and varieties of zoysiagrass that vary widely in color, texture, and establishment rate.

Japanese or **Korean lawngrass** (*Zoysia japonica*) has a very coarse texture like tall fescue, a light green color, a faster growth rate than most zoysias, and excellent cold tolerance. Varieties that can be seeded include **Cathay**, **Companion**, **Sunrise**, **Sunstar**, **Traveler**, and **Zenith**. Japanese lawngrass can be used for lawns or general turf areas where convenience of establishment by seed is more important than quality. This species does not make as good a lawn as other zoysias.

- **Crowne** (*Zoysia japonica* 'Crowne') is a coarse-textured, vegetatively propagated clone of Japanese lawngrass. It is noted for drought tolerance, cold hardiness, and rapid recuperative ability.
- **El Toro** (*Zoysia japonica* 'El Toro') has a coarser leaf texture than Meyer. El Toro establishes faster than Meyer, has better cool-season color, and is less prone to thatch buildup. El Toro is also reported to greenup earlier in the spring and have improved resistance to rust disease. It has good shade tolerance and uses less water than Meyer and Emerald.
- **Empire** and **Empress** are two *Zoysia japonica* selections from Brazil. Empire is a coarse-textured, blue-green colored turfgrass with an open growth habit; it is noted for its ability to cover rapidly and to tolerate rotary mowers. Empress has a blue-green color with leaves that are similar in size to Meyer. It covers more rapidly than Emerald. Because it lacks cold tolerance, Empress should not be grown in the piedmont or mountains.
- **Meyer** (*Zoysia japonica* 'Meyer'), also called Amazoy, has a deep-green color. The leaf is intermediate in width between that of Emerald and Japa-

nese lawngrass. Meyer is the zoysiagrass often advertised as the "miracle" or "wondergrass" in newspapers and magazines. Currently, it is the most widely planted zoysiagrass in the South. Meyer spreads quickly and is the most cold-tolerant. It is less shade-tolerant than Emerald. Establishment is by sod, plugs, or sprigs.
- **Palisades** is a medium-coarse textured vegetatively propagated clone of Meyer. It is noted for its shade tolerance, cold hardiness, and rapid recuperative potential.

Emerald zoysia is a selected hybrid between Japanese lawngrass (*Z. japonica*) and mascarenegrass (*Z. tenuifolia*). This hybrid combines the winter-hardiness, color, and faster growth rate of one parent with the fine texture and density of the other. Emerald's characteristics include very fine leaves, good winter hardiness, shade tolerance, and wear resistance, a moderate rate of spread, and a dark green color. Emerald lacks the cold tolerance of Meyer. Emerald tolerates light shade, but develops thatch rather quickly despite its very slow rate of growth. Emerald may be the most beautiful of the zoysia lawngrasses, but it is subject to thatch buildup. It is susceptible to dollar and leaf spot and brown patch disease. Emerald is a good choice for top quality lawns where time and money allow for adequate maintenance.

Manilagrass (*Zoysia matrella*) produces a finer and denser lawn than Japanese lawngrass, but it is less winter hardy. The thin leaves are sharply pointed and wiry. Manilagrass resembles bermudagrass in texture, color, and quality. It is recommended for a high quality, high maintenance lawn where a slow rate of establishment is not a disadvantage. Cultivars include:
- **Cavalier**, which has a fine texture and good shade and salt tolerance, and good recuperative ability under traffic.
- **Diamond,** a fine-texture vegetatively propagated selection that has good shade and salt tolerance and brown patch resistance.

Additional zoysiagrass cultivars include **Zeon**, **Zorro** and **Zoy-Boy**.

Lawn Establishment

There are four steps to turfgrass establishment: (1) select a turfgrass that is adapted for that particular area; (2) prepare the soil for planting; (3) plant by seed, sod, plugs, or sprigs; and (4) maintain the newly planted lawn to ensure successful establishment and growth.

Turfgrass Selection

Proper turfgrass selection is one of the most important factors in the successful establishment of a home lawn. The lawn grass you select should be adapted to your area and meet the level of lawn quality you desire.

Besides carefully choosing the right turfgrass species, such as hybrid bermudagrass or tall fescue, you must select from among the cultivars of each species. Some turfgrass cultivars perform better than others in South Carolina. Therefore, deciding which cultivar to purchase is an important consideration.

Soil Preparation

The key to establishing a lawn successfully is proper soil preparation. Prepare the soil the same whether planting by seed, sprigs, stolons, or sod.

Soil Test

Soil testing will determine whether the soil pH and nutrient (phosphorus, potassium, calcium, and magnesium) levels are in a range that favor turfgrass growth. The soil test report will indicate how much fertilizer or lime needs to be applied. Lime and fertilizer applications work best when they can be mixed into the upper 4 to 6 inches of the soil. Contact a local county Extension office for a "Record Sheet" and box. See Appendix 1, Soil Testing for instructions on taking a soil sample.

Clean and Rough Grade

Remove all debris from the location to be planted. This includes rocks, bottles, large roots, and old tree trunks. If extensive grading is needed, remove the topsoil and stockpile it for replacement after the rough grade is established. The site should have a gentle slope of 1 to 2% (1 to 2 ft. of fall per 100 ft.) away from the house. The rough grade should conform to the final grade after the topsoil is replaced. Slopes more than 10% should be sodded and not seeded due to erosion problems.

If you want to install an irrigation system, make sure that it is properly designed and installed

Amending heavy, clay soils with sand. Sand modification is only recommended in those instances where drainage is poor or compaction is excessive. It is commonly used on golf course putting greens. However, due to the high cost of proper modification and the need for exact specifications, it is rarely used to modify soil in home lawns. When used, any sand amendment must provide a final mixture containing at least 75% of a medium-sized sand to provide improved aeration. Modification below this level will actually decrease pore space in the soil and decrease turf quality. Turfgrasses grown in a soil that has been extensively modified with sand will likely require more frequent irrigation and fertilization.

according to design specifications. An irrigation system's capacity to perform properly is limited by its design and construction. A poorly designed or improperly installed system will never operate satisfactorily.

Deep Tillage

Rototilling loosens compacted soil and improves the speed and depth of rooting. A tractor-mounted or self-propelled tiller will adequately till the soil. Till in two directions, as deeply as possible, preferably 6 to 8 inches, to ensure a thorough and uniform seedbed mixture.

The subsurface may become compacted during rough grading, especially if the ground is wet. This compacted layer must be broken up. A spring-tooth harrow works well on lightly compacted soils; a small rotovator may be needed for more heavily compacted sites.

Care should be taken not to destroy the existing trees in the lawn. Cutting a large percentage of a tree's roots during soil tillage can severely damage or kill a tree. Trees covering the roots with soil. If additional soil is necessary at a tree base, a "tree well" should be constructed (Figure 2).

Return the topsoil

Once the subsurface is established, spread the stockpiled topsoil. Allow for at least a final depth of 6 to 8 inches after the soil has settled. This translates to spreading about 8 to 10 inches of topsoil over the subgrade. On steep slopes or where rock outcrops exist, at least 12 inches of topsoil are needed for proper maintenance.

Figure 2

Tree well system installed before raising the surrounding soil level to prevent or reduce injury caused by soil fill.

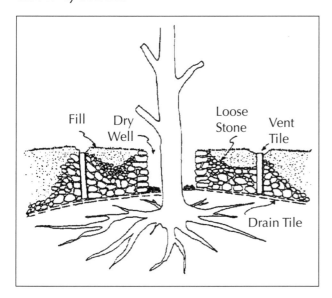

The soil can be improved by adding organic matter (Table 4). Organic matter improves water retention in sandy soils and drainage in clay soils, and reduces fertilizer leaching.

Fertilization and Liming

Apply the amounts of fertilizer and lime recommended by the soil test and work these amounts into the upper 6 to 8 inches of soil.

In the absence of a soil test for all grasses except centipede, which prefers acidic soils and low phosphorus levels, apply 75 lbs. of limestone per 1,000 sq. ft. Also, apply a "starter-type" of fertilizer that contains the higher amounts of phosphate that are required by turfgrass seedlings. Apply 20 to 30 lbs. of a commercial grade fertilizer, such as 5-10-15, 6-18- 18, or 5-10-10 per 1,000 sq. ft. of lawn. If a water-soluble, quick-release source of nitrogen is used, do not apply more than $1\frac{1}{2}$ lbs. of actual nitrogen per 1,000 sq. ft. If a water-insoluble, slow-release source of nitrogen is used, such as urea-formaldehyde, you can apply 3 to 5 lbs. of actual nitrogen per 1,000 sq. ft. prior to planting.

Final Grading

Delay final grading and incorporation of the fertilizer until right before planting time. If this is done too far in advance, some fertilizer may be leached out and the soil may become crusted. After the fertilizer and lime have been worked into the soil, the soil should be firmed by rolling with a water ballast roller before seeding, sodding, and plugging (Figure 3). Do not pulverize the soil. The best soil for seeding has a granular texture with small clods of soil varying from $\frac{1}{8}$ inch to $\frac{3}{4}$ inch in size. However, if the area is to be sprigged the soil should remain loose in the upper 2 to 3 inches so a portion of each sprig can be "set" or pushed into the soil. On light sandy soils firm the seedbed before planting to help prevent the soil from drying out. Now it is time to plant.

Seeding

Three primary factors that affect turfgrass establishment from seed are planting procedures, mulching, and care after seeding.

Successful establishment from seed depends on purchasing top quality seed. South Carolina law requires that each container of seed have a tag listing the turfgrass species and variety, purity, percent germination, and weed content. A typi-

Table 4

Soil amendments and their rate of application for incorporating into turfgrass soils.

Material	Volume (cubic yd. per 1,000 sq. ft.)	Depth (inches) before soil incorporation (6 to 8 inch depth)
Composted sludge[a]	3 to 6	1 to 2
Sawdust[b]	3 to 6	1 to 2
Composted yard trimmings	3 to 6	1 to 2
Sphagnum peat moss	3	1
Rotted farm manure[a]	3	1
Gypsum (calcium sulfate)	100 lbs.	–

[a]With composted sludge and farm manure, do not apply additional nitrogen at establishment.
[b]Additional nitrogen will be required with the use of sawdust. Incorporate 40 lbs. of 10-10-10 per 1,000 sq. ft. with the sawdust *in lieu* of standard fertilization recommendations.

Figure 3

Firming and smoothing the seedbed with a water-ballast roller.

cal seed label contains the following information (Figure 4):

Variety—Each kind or variety of lawn seed is listed by its purity ("Pure Seed"), which is the amount of desired seed expressed as a percentage of the total weight of the box or bag. Look for seed that has a purity of 90% or higher. Also, look for specific trade names of varieties rather than the generic names or kinds, such as "tall fescue." For example, on the sample label, Jaguar II, Tribute, and Rebel Jr. are trade name improved turf-type fescue varieties.

Germination—The germination figure is a very important percentage because it tells you how much of each variety of pure seed will "sprout" to produce a grass plant. In the example, the turf-type tall fescues germination rate is 85% . The higher the percentage, the better.

To help you compare different lots of seed, calculate the percentage of pure live seed. To do this, multiply the percentage of Pure Seed by the percentage of Germination. For example, the germination rate on our sample tag is 85% and the amount of pure seed is 99.55. Then, 85% of the seed will produce normal plants. Note: If you want to do the math, here's the equation: ([.85 x .9955] x 100 = 84.62%).

Other Crop Seed—If there are any kinds of lawn seed other than those listed under "Variety," it will be listed on the label by weight percentage. These "off types" of seed are not specifically named, but they can detract from the appearance of the lawn. In our example, "Other Crop Seed" is 0.26%, or about $\frac{1}{4}$ of 1 percent by weight. This is certainly acceptable. The lower the percentage, the better when evaluating or comparing seed labels.

Inert matter—This is any substance in the box or bag that is not capable of growing. It could be broken seed that could not be cleaned out, sand, chaff, or even filler that's added to take up space. In our example, the inert matter is listed at 0.9%—certainly an acceptable level. The lower the percentage of inert matter, the better.

Weed Seed—If any weed seed is present, it is listed by percentage of weight. Although we don't want to buy any weeds seeds with our lawn seeds, it is very difficult and expensive to catch all the weed seeds during the cleaning process. Acceptable limits range from 0.3% to 0.5%. In our example, 0.10% is well below the acceptable level. The higher the percentage of weed seed shown on the label, the poorer the quality of the box or bag you are buying.

Noxious Weeds—The S.C. Dept. of Agriculture maintains a list of weeds that are so troublesome

Figure 4

Typical turfgrass seed label.

LOT NO. 1003
ACME Brand Tall Fescue Blend

Pure Seed	Variety	Kind	Germination	Origin
40%	Jaguar II	Tall Fescue	85%	Oregon
35%	Tribute	Tall Fescue	85%	Oregon
24.55%	Rebel Jr.	Tall Fescue	85%	Canada

0.26% OTHER CROP SEED   TEST DATE: 6/01
0.09% INERT MATTER   NET WEIGHT: 50 pounds
0.10% WEED SEED
NOXIOUS WEED SEED: None found per pound

ACME Superduper Seed Co., Anytown, SC 29634

and undesirable that their presence must be stated on the seed label. For a quality lawn, avoid labelled boxes, bags, or bins that contain noxious weeds.

Other Information—The name of the produce/distributor, where each variety was grown (Origin), lot number used for tracing the container through marketing channels, and when the seed lot was tested. South Carolina state law requires that a bag or box be retested and relabeled after 9 months if not sold. You should check and be aware of the month and year the seed was tested.

In short, read the label and buy quality seed, especially improved lawn varieties with insect, disease, and drought resistance. Proper seeding rates and times for turf-grasses are listed in Table 5.

Many seeding methods are used, ranging from sowing by hand to using mechanical equipment for large turf areas. Evenness of seed distribution is important from the standpoint of overall uniformity. The seedbed should be well-prepared and leveled. Rake the entire area with a garden rake. Seed should be applied mechanically either with a drop-type or rotary spreader. Mechanical seeders provide a more uniform distribution of seed than hand seeding. For best distribution of seed, sow one-half the required amount in one direction and apply the remainder at right angles to the first seeding (Figure 5). For very small seed like centipedegrass or ber-

Figure 5

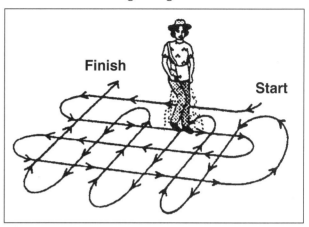

Divide the quantity of seed into two equal parts, and spread half the seed in one direction and the other half at a right angle to the first.

mudagrass, it may be helpful to mix the seed with a carrier such as corn meal, grits, or an organic fertilizer to distribute the seed evenly. When mixing seed with a carrier, make sure that the seed and carrier remain thoroughly mixed during application.

With a rake, mix the grass seed with the top $\frac{1}{4}$ inch of soil. Then roll the seedbed with a light or empty water-ballast roller to ensure good seed-to-soil contact. Mulch the seedbed to prevent soil erosion, retain moisture, and prevent crusting of the soil surface. The most commonly used mulch is straw. However, it is important to use weed-free straw.

Table 5

Seeding rates of lawn grasses.

Grass	Pounds per per 1,000 sq. ft	Planting Time	Days to Germinate
Kentucky bluegrass[a]	2 to 3	September, October is best; early spring is second best	6 to 30
Red fescue[a]	3 to 5	Same as above	14
Ryegrass[b], Annual	5 to 10	September to November	3 to 7
Ryegrass, Perennial	5 to 10	Same as above	3 to 7
Tall fescue/Turf Type[a]	5 to 8 / 4 to 6	September, October is best; early spring is second best	6 to 12
Bahiagrass (scarified)	7 to 10 (scarified)	April to July	7 to 21
Carpetgrass	3 to 5	April to July	10 to 20
Centipedegrass	$\frac{1}{4}$ to $\frac{1}{2}$	April to July	10 to 20
Common bermudagrass			
--hulled	2	April to July	10 to 20
--unhulled	4	Fall	14 to 21
Japanese lawngrass (*Zoysia japonica*)	$\frac{1}{2}$ to 3	May to July	10 to 14

[a]Late spring and early summer seedings of cool-season grasses usually result in failure. If spring or early summer seeding is necessary, as much as 50% of the grass may die during the heat of summer because the root system is not properly developed. Turfgrass can be replanted in the fall to improve the stand.
[b]Ryegrass is used as an overseeding on cool-season grasses to produce green color during the winter.

One bale of straw (60 to 80 lbs.) will cover about 1,000 sq. ft. Use enough weed-free straw so that 50 to 75% of the bare ground is protected. Straw can be removed when the turf reaches a height of 1 to $1\frac{1}{2}$ inches or can be left to decompose if it is not spread too thickly. Peat moss or aged sawdust does not make a good mulch for seeded lawns. These materials compete with the seed for water and are slow to decay.

Water the lawn as soon as possible after seeding. Watering with a fine spray will help seed to germinate, but be sure to prevent washing or puddling. Frequent watering is essential until the seedlings become established.

Care of the Newly Seeded Lawn

The first 2 or 3 months of a newly seeded lawn are critical to its successful establishment. You should pay particular attention to watering, fertilizing, and mowing.

Watering. Proper watering is the most critical step in establishing turfgrasses from seed. Failure to provide the newly seeded lawn with enough moisture is one of the main reasons for poor establishment.

Supply water frequently (quantity is less a factor at this time) to keep the soil moist but not waterlogged. Water two or three times a day in small quantities for about 2 to 3 weeks will ensure adequate moisture for germination.

If the surface of the soil is allowed to dry out any time after the seeds have begun to swell and before roots have developed, many of the seedlings will die.

Initial watering should be from a fine spray, if possible, or from sprinklers with a low precipitation rate. Coarse spray and high water pressure or high precipitation rates will erode the soil and wash away the seeds.

Water lightly and frequently so the seedlings do not dry out. The goal is to water often enough to keep the seedbed moist but not saturated, until the plants can develop sufficient root systems to take advantage of deeper and less frequent watering. Soils that have not been mulched will tend to dry out quickly. Under these conditions, frequent irrigation will be required. Less irrigation will be needed if a mulch was used. The quantity of water applied will be small and should be maintained for at least 3 weeks following planting.

As the seedlings mature and their roots develop, reduce the number of waterings but increase the volume of water to moisten the entire root zone, not just the soil surface.

Fertilization. A light application of nitrogen fertilizer made when the seedlings are between $1\frac{1}{2}$ and 2 inches tall will enhance the establishment rate substantially. Apply about $\frac{1}{2}$ lb. of actual nitrogen per 1,000 sq. ft., such as 3 lbs. of 16-4-8, and water it into the soil. Avoid applying excessively high levels of nitrogen which will restrict root, rhizome, and stolon growth, and will encourage disease outbreaks.

Mowing. Begin normal mowing practices when the turfgrass seedlings reach a height that is one-third higher than the normal mowing height. Once you start mowing, mow routinely at a constant cutting height. Do not allow the seedlings to reach an excessively tall height before cutting them back. Newly germinated turfgrass seedlings, which have a small, shallow root system, can be easily pulled out of the ground by mowing. Maintain a sharp cutting blade to help prevent these seedlings from being removed from the soil.

Weed control. Timing of weed control practices is also critically important once seeds have germinated. Most herbicides are somewhat toxic to newly germinated turfgrass plants. Postemergence applications of a herbicide for weed control should be delayed as long as possible after seeding. Refer to the pesticide label instructions for the appropriate time of application.

Vegetative Planting

Vegetative planting is simply the transplanting of large or small pieces of grass. Solid sodding covers the entire seedbed with vegetation. Spot sodding, plugging, sprigging, or stolonizing refer to the planting of pieces of sod or individual stems or underground runners.

Most warm-season turfgrasses are established by planting vegetative plant parts. Exceptions include carpetgrass centipedegrass, common bermudagrass, and Japanese lawngrass (*Zoysia japonica*), which can be established from seed.

Sodding

Sodding is more expensive than sprigging or plugging, but it produces a so-called "instant" lawn. Sodding is expensive but is recommended where quick cover is desired for aesthetic reasons or to prevent soil erosion. Sodding permits the establishment of a high quality turf in the shortest time.

Establishment procedures for sod include soil preparation, obtaining sod of high quality, transplanting, and postplanting care.

Soil Preparation

Soil preparation for sodding is identical to that for seeding.

Sod Quality

Before buying the sod, inspect it carefully for weeds, diseases, and insects. Store the sod in a cool, shady place until used, but do not store it for a long period. Purchase the right amount and try to install it as soon as it is delivered.

Sodding

The primary objective in transplanting sod is to achieve quick rooting or "knitting" into the underlying soil. To speed up rooting, prepare the soil properly, keep the soil moist, and prevent the sod from drying out.

Sod of cool- and warm-season grasses can be installed anytime during the year. However, summer-sodding of cool-season grasses is discouraged because of heat and moisture stress. When sodding in the summer, moisten the soil before laying the sod to avoid placing the turf roots in contact with excessively dry and hot soil. Also, have irrigation available. *Winter* or *dormant sodding* of warm-season grasses is a routine commercial practice even though the chances for survival are riskier than when sodding during the growing season.

When installing sod, establish a straight line lengthwise through the lawn area. The sod can then be laid on either side of the line with the ends staggered in a checkerboard fashion (Figure 6). A sharpened concrete trowel is handy for cutting pieces, forcing the sod tight, but not overlapping, and leveling small depressions.

Do not stretch the sod while laying. The sod will shrink upon drying and cause voids. Stagger lateral joints to promote more uniform growth and strength. On steep slopes, lay the sod across the angle of the slope; it may be necessary to peg the sod to the soil with stakes to keep it from sliding. Immediately after the sod has been transplanted, it is important to roll or tamp it (Figure 7). This will eliminate any air spaces between the soil and the sod. Roots will not grow through an air space to reach the soil. Rolling should be done perpendicular to the direction the sod was laid.

Water newly transplanted sod immediately to wet the soil below to a 3-inch depth to enhance rooting. Do not let the soil dry out until a good union between the sod and soil surface has been

Figure 6

Place the sod pieces tightly together in a staggered, checkerboard pattern, similar to bricks in a wall.

achieved. To smooth out the lawn surface, apply light, frequent applications of soil topdressing.

Post-transplant Care

Newly transplanted sod should be irrigated similar to a newly seeded area. Water to a depth of 3 inches immediately after transplanting to promote deep root growth. In the absence of adequate rainfall, water daily or as often as necessary to keep the soil moist. When the sod starts to root into the underlying soil, water more deeply and thoroughly.

Do not mow until the sod is firmly rooted and securely in place. The mowing height and frequency on newly sodded areas should be the same as normally practiced on established turfs. Fertilizer should not be needed, since the grass should have

Figure 7

Roll freshly laid sod pieces to ensure good sod-to-soil contact.

been grown under optimum conditions and fertilizer should have been incorporated into the soil before sodding. A fertility program can be started after the sod has established a good root system.

Plugging

The planting of 2- to 4-inch diameter square, circular, or block-shaped pieces of sod at regular intervals is called **plugging**. Three to 10 times as much planting material is necessary for plugging as sprigging (Table 6). This procedure can be used to repair damaged areas in the lawn or for lawn establishment. Establishing a lawn using turfgrass plugs can be done successfully where the cost of solid sodding is prohibitive. The most common turfgrasses that are started by the use of plugs are centipedegrass, St. Augustinegrass, and zoysiagrass (Figure 8). These plugs are planted into prepared soil on 6- or 12-inch centers; i.e., 6 or 12 inches from the center of one plug to the center of the next one (Figure 9). The closer the plugs are planted together, the faster the sod will cover. However, the closer the plugs are planted together, the more sod it will take to provide plugs to cover the lawn.

Prior to plugging, prepare the soil the same as that for seeding or sodding. Plugging can be accomplished by special machines designed to plant plugs or by hand on smaller areas. Timing of plug transplanting for warm-season turfgrasses should take place in the late spring or early summer. This will give the turf optimum growing conditions for

Figure 8

Establishing a new lawn by plugs.

successful establishment. After the plugs have been transplanted, roll the planting bed to ensure good plant-to-soil contact. Water following the same guidelines as for sodding.

Post-plugging care involves mowing at the recommended height and frequency required for that particular turfgrass. Fertilizing 3 to 4 weeks after plugging and watering properly will also enhance establishment.

Sprigging and Stolonizing

The best quality bermudagrass, St. Augustinegrass, and zoysiagrass must be planted vegetatively using sod, plugs, or sprigs. **Sprigging** is the planting of stolons or rhizomes in furrows or small holes. A sprig is an individual stem or piece of stem of grass without any adhering soil. As long as a sprig has at least one node or joint, it has the potential of developing into a grass plant. A suitable sprig should have two to four nodes from which roots can develop. The sprigs are prepared by mechanical shredding or hand-tearing of sod into individual sprigs, or purchased by the bushel (most commonly bermudagrass). Sprigs have little or no soil from the area where they were harvested so they are ideal for an area where soil contamination is not wanted. Soil preparation for sprigging should be the same as for the other methods of planting.

To plant sprigs, dig furrows 8 to 12 inches apart and place the sprigs at a one- to two-inch depth (use the shallower depth if

Table 6

Plugging and sprigging rates for warm-season grasses.

Turfgrass	Spacing (inches)	Amount of sod (sq. ft.)/ 1,000 sq. ft.[*]
Bermudagrass		
--2-in. plugs	12	30 to 50
--sprigs	12	2 to 5
Centipede		
--2-in. plugs	6	100 to 150
--sprigs	6	30 to 50
St. Augustine		
--2-in. plugs	6 to 12	30 to 50
--sprigs	6 to 12	10 to 15
Zoysiagrass		
--2-in. plugs	6	100 to 150
--sprigs	6	8 to 15

[*]Based on estimates of 1 sq. ft. of sod = 80 linear ft. of sprigs; 1 sq. yd. of sod = 1 bushel of sprigs; and 1 sq. yd. of sod yields 324 two-inch plugs. The numbers in the column refer to the number of square feet of sod from which either two-inch plugs or sprigs can be obtained.

Figure 9

Plugs are normally spaced on 6- to 12-inch centers.

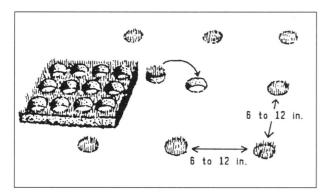

adequate moisture is available) every 4 to 6 inches in the furrows. The closer the sprigs are, the faster the grass will cover the soil. After placing the sprigs in the furrow, cover a part of the sprig with soil and firm. The leaves should be left exposed at the soil surface (Figure 10). This can be done with a roller or by stepping on the soil around the sprig. Water as soon as possible after planting.

Another method is to place the sprigs on the soil surface at the desired interval end-to-end, about 6 inches apart, and then press one end of the sprig into the soil with a notched stick or blunt piece of metal like a dull shovel. A portion of the sprig should be left above ground exposed to light.

Regardless of the planting method, each sprig should be tamped or rolled firmly into the soil. Since the sprigs are planted at a shallow depth, they are very prone to drying out. Light, frequent waterings are necessary until roots become well-established. Watering lightly once or twice daily will be required for several weeks after planting. Mulching can also be used in vegetative planting for moisture conservation and erosion control.

Stolonizing is the broadcasting of stolons on the soil surface and covering by topdressing or pressing into the soil (Figure 11). Stolonizing requires more planting material but will produce a quicker cover than sprigs. It is extremely important to maintain a moist surface during the establishment period. The soil surface can become quite dry in a relatively short period of time, especially on sandy soils. Allowing the soil surface to dry will cause the sprigs or stolons to dry out.

Seed vs. Sod

A quality lawn containing recommended mixtures and species can be established with either seed or sod. Initially, seed is less expensive than sod. However, successful establishment is more risky with seed than with sod, and often when reseeding areas where soil erosion is likely, overall expense may be less with sod. Sodding nearly eliminates the chances for failure where erosion is a concern.

Sodding saves establishment time and provides a functional and aesthetic turf where weed infestations will not be an immediate problem. When using seed, a weed control program must be implemented to reduce the weed competition. Sod offers less time limitations in that it may be established during any season, even in summer or winter, if irrigation is available.

Figure 10

In sprigging, leave $^1/_3$ to $^1/_4$ of each sprig above ground and 4 to 6 inches apart in the furrow.

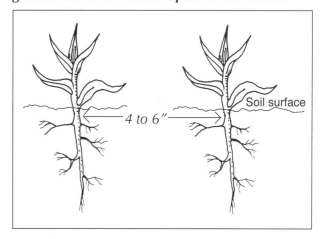

Figure 11

Broadcasting fresh stolons on a prepared soil surface.

Lawn Renovation

Renovation is the improvement of a turfgrass stand without completely starting all over from scratch. **Reestablishment** refers to completely replacing the old lawn with a new one. Turfgrass renovation is necessary when the existing turfgrass has declined to a point where cultural practices will not revive the turf, but complete reestablishment is unnecessary. Generally, if more than half of the area comprises desirable turf, renovation will succeed.

Several factors can cause turfgrass to deteriorate, including improper mowing, watering, and fertilizing, poor drainage, soil compaction, excessive thatch, incorrect pesticide usage, and lawn pests such as insects or weeds. Sometimes problems relate to growing an unadapted grass species, excessive shade, tree and shrub root competition, or winter injury. Excessive shade and tree/shrub root problems can be solved by replacing the lawn grasses with mulch or a shade-tolerant groundcover or mulch.

Timing

Cool-season turfgrasses are best renovated in early fall (September to October) at the beginning of their growing season. Trying to reestablish a cool-season turfgrass in the spring will not allow the lawn to mature before summer stresses appear. Warm-season turfgrasses are best renovated in the spring or early summer (April to June). Renovating warm-season grasses in the fall often results in winter-damaged turf.

Step-by-step Renovation Process

Step 1. Determine what caused the lawn to fail. Planting grass into a problem area without understanding the cause of its failure may result in another failed lawn.

Step 2. Soil test. Base fertilizer and lime applications on soil test results. Contact a county Extension agent for soil sampling information.

Step 3. Eliminate all undesirable weeds or turfgrass species. Identify the weeds for proper control. Contact Clemson University's Home and Garden Information Center (HGIC) at http://hgic.clemson.edu or 1-888-656-9988 for help in weed identification and control recommendations. Be aware that some weed control chemicals require a waiting period between the time of herbicide application and planting. Follow the herbicide label instructions for information about proper handling and application.

Step 4. Mow and rake. Mow the area lower than normal and remove the clippings, leaves, and other debris by sweeping or raking.

Step 5. Remove excessive thatch. Thatch is a layer of partially decomposed plant material that builds up on the soil surface. Usually more than $1/2$ inch of thatch on general turf areas decreases turf vigor by restricting the movement of air, water, fertilizer, and pesticides into the soil. Excessive thatch also restricts root development and provides a suitable environment for insect and disease pests. Mechanically remove thatch with a vertical mower or a power rake. This equipment can often be rented from rental companies. Refer to the section titled "Thatch Development and Control" for more information.

Step 6. Till or core compacted soil. Cultivate the soil by tilling or coring ("aerifying") to "loosen" compacted soil. A coring machine which removes a soil core is most effective. After coring use a vertical mower to help break up the soil cores brought to the surface. Coring is most effective when the soil is moist because the tines will penetrate deeply.

Step 7. Add fertilizer and lime according to soil test recommendations.

Step 8. Seed, sod, plug, or sprig new grass into the area. You may want to adjust the planting rates to agree with the percentage already in turf. For example, if 50% of the area has good turf, reduce the recommended planting rate in half. Be sure to get good seed-to-soil contact when sowing seed. Rake the seed into the soil or cover it by topdressing with a thin layer ($1/4$ inch) of soil. When seeding into lawn grasses, drag the seed into the slits using an old carpet. Afterwards, firm the soil by lightly rolling. Where there is little existing grass or where erosion may be a problem, use a light mulch. Some available rental machines cultivate and plant in a single operation. Vegetative materials (sprigs or plugs) need to be planted into the soil. On small areas, use an axe or trowel to make a small opening for sprig or plug placement. Place sprigs or plugs 6 to 12 inches apart and firm the soil around them after placement. Any technique that places part of the sprig or plug below the soil surface is suitable.

Step 9. Water. Apply water immediately after planting and keep the soil moist, not wet, until the seedlings or sprigs become well-established. This usually requires light, daily waterings for 2 to 3 weeks.

Step 10. Mow the grass when it reaches $1^1/_2$ times its recommended height.

Basic Lawn Management

Lawn quality can be ranked as "average" or "above-average." An average quality lawn requires only basic maintenance, such as mowing, liming if needed, and fertilizing. This type of lawn may have several types of grasses and some weeds. An average quality lawn can be obtained with a minimum of money, time, and effort. An above-average or superior quality lawn requires additional care, like weed, disease, and insect control. You can do it yourself or you can purchase these services through a lawn service company. Generally, lawns in the above-average quality range have a dense population of lawn grasses with a minimum number of weeds.

Whatever level of quality you desire, the final product should be a healthy, dense lawn. A well-maintained lawn will prevent soil erosion, enrich the soil, and act as a living filter for water as it passes through the soil.

By correctly carrying out basic lawn maintenance practices, you can reduce the need for supplementary practices like pest control.

Soil Testing

One of the first steps in producing and maintaining an attractive lawn is to obtain an analysis of a representative soil sample from the lawn area. Instructions for taking soil samples and submitting soil samples for analysis by the Clemson Soil Testing Laboratory are in Appendix 1 and on the soil sample bag.

Proper sampling is important to ensure representative soil test results and proper fertilizer recommendations. Once the soil has been analyzed, your Clemson Extension office will mail you a report with the plant nutrient levels and fertilizer and lime recommendations.

Soil test results supply a wealth of information concerning the nutritional status of a soil and may aid in the detection of potential problems that could limit turfgrass growth. Also, soil testing protects against the expense and environmental hazards resulting from excessive fertilizer applications. A typical soil test supplies information about soil pH, lime requirements, phosphorus, potassium, calcium, magnesium, zinc, and manganese (see Appendix 1). The nitrogen requirements of the turfgrass cannot be reliably evaluated by a soil test. Therefore, the soil test report will not contain a nitrogen recommendation. For nitrogen applications on cool- and warm-season lawns, follow the suggested fertilization schedule in Table 9.

Soil Acidity and Alkalinity

The acidity or alkalinity of a soil, expressed as pH, affects a plant's ability to absorb fertilizers and other nutrients present in the soil. Most lawn grasses grow well when the soil pH is between 5.8 and 6.5; carpetgrass and centipedegrass prefers a pH between 5.5 and 6.0 (Table 7). A pH either too low or too high will reduce the availability of plant nutrients. Therefore, it is very important that you maintain a proper soil pH.

Normally, liming materials are used to increase soil pH and supply the essential nutrients of calcium and magnesium. The two most commonly available liming materials are calcitic and dolomitic limestones. In instances where the soil tests low in magnesium, dolomitic limestone should be used. Generally, it takes about six months for calcitic and dolomitic limestone to have their maximum effect on soil acidity.

The amount of lime required to properly adjust the soil pH depends on the kinds of lawn grasses being grown, soil type, and current soil pH. The greater the amount of organic matter or clay in the soil, the more lime is required to change the pH. Apply the proper amount of lime according to soil test results.

Table 7			

Lawn grasses best adapted for various soil pH levels.

pH			
5 to 5.4	**5.5 to 5.9**	**6 to 6.4**	**6.5 to 6.9**
Bermudagrass	Bermudagrass	Bermudagrass	Bermudagrass
Carpetgrass	Carpetgrass	Bluegrass	Bluegrass
Centipedegrass	Centipedegrass	Fescue	Fescue
Bahiagrass	Bahiagrass	Italian ryegrass	Perennial ryegrass
	Italian ryegrass	Perennial ryegrass	St. Augustinegrass
	Fine fescue	St. Augustinegrass	Zoysiagrass
		Zoysiagrass	

Credit: L. B. McCarty, 2003, Southern Lawns.

Fertilizing

Understanding the nutritional requirements of your lawn and soil nutrient levels are perhaps the most important aspects to producing a quality stand of turfgrass. Fertilization of lawns is essential for the production of quality turf. However, exceeding recommended fertilizer application rates or improper application timing can pollute surface water and groundwater quality.

Lawn fertilization is the application of sufficient amounts of all essential elements to produce optimum turf growth. Lawns require the **macronutrients** nitrogen, phosphorous, and potassium in the greatest quantities. They should be applied as recommended by soil test results. Nutrients needed in minor quantities and applied less frequently are calcium, magnesium, and sulfur. These minor elements are usually present in a large enough quantity in the soil that they do not need to be added with a fertilizer. The **micronutrients** iron, manganese, zinc, copper, molybdenum, chlorine, boron, and nickel are required in very small quantities and are applied less often than the macronutrients. Micronutrients are as essential as the major elements, but are required in microamounts. Tissue testing is the usual means by which minor elements are quantified and micronutrient deficiencies are revealed.

Nitrogen

Nitrogen is probably the most important element you can apply which affects plant growth. Nitrogen will affect a turfgrass in several ways, including color, density, shoot and root growth, susceptibility to diseases and insects, environmental stresses, and its ability to recover after it has been damaged. A nitrogen fertility program should allow for a slow, steady growth. Applying excessive amounts of nitrogen will encourage shoot growth at the expense of root growth, causing a reduction root growth. Fertilizing with high levels of nitrogen will also increase the incidence of diseases and thatch accumulation. It will also make the turf more prone to winter damage.

Several factors influence the nitrogen requirements of your lawn, including the species of grass being grown, the soil type, and environmental conditions. The timing of a nitrogen application is also critical to the development of a lawn. Fertilizing warm-season turfgrasses too early in the spring with high levels of nitrogen can cause a reduction in root growth as the plants emerge from dormancy. Fertilizing these grasses too late in the fall may increase the chance of winter damage. Cool-season turf-grasses should be fertilized with nitrogen during the fall and early spring. Fertilizing these grasses with nitrogen during the summer will increase the chances of disease problems.

Nitrogen Availability

The source of nitrogen in fertilizers influences nitrogen availability and turf response. There are two categories of nitrogen sources: **quick-release** and **slow-release**. **Quick-release** materials are water soluble, can be readily used by the plant, are susceptible to leaching, and have a relatively short period of response. Quick-release sources include ammonium nitrate, urea, ammonium sulfate, and calcium nitrate (Table 8).

Slow-release nitrogen sources release their nitrogen over extended periods of time, and are applied less frequently and at somewhat higher rates than the quickly available nitrogen sources. When properly applied, they also reduce the chances of fertilizer "burn" that is common with ammonium nitrate and urea. Fertilizer burn is the brownish discoloration that occurs on grass blades as a result of coming into contact with a soluble fertilizer. It can be minimized by watering the lawn immediately after fertilizing. Slow-release sources are less susceptible to leaching and are preferred on sandy soils, which tend to leach. They are a good choice for areas where the potential of runoff is very high such as slopes, compacted soil, or sparsely covered lawns; since the nutrients are released slowly, the potential for runoff and water contamination is less. Slow-release sources include urea formaldehyde (UF), UF-based products (methylene ureas), sulfur-coated urea (SCU), isobutylidene diurea (IBDU), natural organics (bone meal, fish meal, dried blood, and animal manures), and activated sewage sludge.

If a fertilizer contains a slow-release nitrogen source, it will be listed on the label as **Water Insoluble Nitrogen** or **W.I.N.** (Figure 12). If W.I.N. is not listed on the fertilizer label, assume that it is all water-soluble or quickly available nitrogen.

The higher the amount of W.I.N., the more slowly released will be the nitrogen. Select a slow-release fertilizer that has at least one-half of the total amount of nitrogen in a water insoluble form.

Products containing slow-release sources of nutrients usually have one or more of the follow-

What the Fertilizer Numbers Mean

Fertilizers are often described by analysis, or three numbers, such as 10-10-10 or 16-4-8. These three numbers give the percent by weight of nitrogen (N), phosphate (P_2O_5), and potash (K_2O). For example, in a 16-4-8 fertilizer, nitrogen makes up 16 percent of the weight, phosphate—which supplies phosphorus— accounts for 4 percent, and potash, a source of potassium, makes up 8 percent of the total weight of fertilizer. The remaining weight of fertilizer (the total must add up to 100 percent) comprises a nutrient carrier. A fertilizer containing all three nutrients, such as a 16-4-8, is referred to as a "complete" fertilizer. If soil tests indicate high levels of phosphorus and potassium, then apply only a fertilizer supplying nitrogen, such as 16-0-0.

The fertilizer ratio of a 16-4-8 fertilizer is 4:1:2. Similarly, a 14-7-14 analysis has a 2:1:2 ratio. Generally, mature lawns require equivalent levels of nitrogen and potassium, especially on sandy soils; therefore, ratios of 4:1:4 or 4:1:3 are recommended.

If a soil test indicates additional phosphate or potash is needed, it may be applied with a complete fertilizer or in separate applications from phosphate or potassium fertilizers. Fertilizers normally used to correct severe phosphorus and/or potassium deficiencies are 0-15-30, 0-12-0, 0-0-53, or 0-0-60. Never apply more than 3 pounds of 0-0-54 or 0-0-60 per 1,000 sq. ft. to an established turf without watering afterwards to prevent foliar burn.

Table 8

A guide to rate of fertilizer materials to use on lawns.

Nitrogen Fertilizers	%N	Pounds needed to supply 1 pound of actual nitrogen per 1,000 sq. ft. of lawn
Quick-release N (inorganics)		
Nitrate of soda	16	6
Nitrate of soda-potash	15	7
Nitrate of potash	13	8
Calcium nitrate	15.5	7
Ammonium nitrate	33.5	3
Ammonium nitrate + lime	18	5
Ammonium sulfate	20.5	5
Mono-ammonium phosphate	11-48-0	9
Diammonium phospate	18-46-0	5.5
Quick-release N (organics)		
Urea	45-47	2
Cyanamid	21	5
Slow-release N (natural organics)		
Sewage sludge	6	16
Castor pomace	4-6	25-16
Cottonseed meal	7	15
Processed tankages	5-10	20-10
Garbage tankage	2-3	40-30
Slow-release N (synthetics)		
Ureaform	38	2.5
Nitroform	38	2
IBDU	31	3
Sulfur-coated urea	36	3
Polymer-/Plastic-/Resin-coated urea	varies	varies

CAUTION: Practically all inorganic fertilizers can "burn" lawn grasses. These materials should be applied when temperatures are cool and watered into the lawn immediately after application. When using slow-release sources of nitrogen, 2 pounds of N can be safely applied per 1,000 sq. ft. per application.

Table 9

Suggested maintenance fertilization schedule for South Carolina lawns.

Lawngrass	Maintenance Level	J	F	M	A	M	J	J	A	S	O	N	D	Total Pounds of N/1,000 sq.ft./year
Piedmont and Mountains														
Bermudagrass	High	--	--	N*	--	C	N	N	C	--	N*	--	N*	3-6
	Low	--	--	--	--	C	N	--	C	--	--	--	--	1-3
Kentucky Bluegrass	High	--	C	--	--	--	--	--	--	C	--	C	--	2-3
	Low	--	C	--	--	--	--	--	--	C	--	--	--	1-2
Carpetgrass	High	--	--	--	--	C	--	--	C	--	--	--	--	1-2
	Low	--	--	--	--	C	--	--	--	--	--	--	--	0-1
Centipedegrass	High	--	--	--	Fe	C	Fe	--	C	--	--	--	--	1-2
	Low	--	--	--	Fe	C	Fe	--	--	--	--	--	--	0-1
St. Augustinegrass	High	--	--	--	Fe	C	N+	--	C	Fe	--	--	--	2-3
	Low	--	--	--	Fe	C	Fe	--	C	--	--	--	--	1-2
Tall Fescue	High	--	C	--	--	--	--	--	--	C	--	C	--	2-3
	Low	--	C	--	--	--	--	--	--	C	--	--	--	1-2
Zoysiagrass	High	--	--	N*	--	C	N	--	C	--	N*	--	--	2-5
	Low	--	--	--	--	C	--	--	C	--	--	--	--	1-3
Sandhills and Coastal Plain														
Bahiagrass	High	--	--	Fe	C	Fe	N	--	C	Fe	--	--	--	2-4
	Low	--	--	--	C	--	Fe	--	C	Fe	--	--	--	1-2
Bermudagrass	High	--	N*	--	C	N	N	N	C	--	N*	--	N*	4-6
	Low	--	--	--	C	--	N	N	C	--	--	--	--	2-3
Carpetgrass	High	--	--	--	C	--	N	--	C	--	--	--	--	1-3
	Low	--	--	--	C	--	--	--	C	--	--	--	--	½-1
Centipedegrass	High	--	--	Fe	C	--	Fe	--	C	Fe	--	--	--	1-2
	Low	--	--	Fe	C	--	Fe	--	C	Fe	--	--	--	½-1
St. Augustinegrass	High	--	--	--	C	N+	N+	--	C	--	--	--	--	2-4
	Low	--	--	--	C	--	Fe	--	C	--	--	--	--	1-2
Zoysiagrass	High	--	N*	--	C	--	N	--	C	--	N*	--	N*	3-5
	Low	--	--	--	C	--	--	--	C	--	--	--	--	1-3

C = Apply a complete fertilizer (such as 16-4-8 or 12-4-8) at 1 lb. N/1,000 sq. ft. for high maintenance lawns or ½ lb. N per 1,000 sq. ft. for low maintenance lawns. An additional potassium application at 1 lb. K per 1,000 sq. ft. in late August through mid-September may increase turfgrass winter hardiness. Phosphorus is normally not needed on established centipedegrass lawns unless recommended by soil test results.

N = Water-soluble inorganic nitrogen source, such as ammonium nitrate or ammonium sulfate, is applied at 1 lb. N/1,000 sq. ft. for higher maintenance lawns and ½ lb. N/1,000 sq.ft. for low maintenance lawns.

Fe = apply iron to provide dark green color without stimulating excessive grass growth. Ferrous sulfate (2 oz. in 3 to 5 gal. water per 1,000 sq. ft.) or a chelated iron source may be used when temperatures are ≤ 80° F and good soil moisture present.

N* = overseeded with ryegrass for winter color. Apply ½ lb. N per 1,000 sq. ft.

N⁺ = To reduce chinch bug problems, use a slow-release N source during the summer.

NOTES:
(1) Total yearly nitrogen rates listed per 1,000 sq. ft. are suggested guidelines. Actual rates depend on the desire aesthetics and location. Those desiring optimum aesthetics may choose the higher rates. The higher rate range also may be needed for lawns located in sandy soils and/or those with longer growing seasons nearer the coast.
(2) Fertilizing centipedegrass in excess of 2 lbs. N per 1,000 sq. ft. yearly is not normally recommended as this often results in the disease/winterkill phenomena called "centipedegrass decline" due to excessive thatch. Also, once established, centipedegrass should not receive additional phosphorus fertilizer unless soil tests suggest otherwise.
(3) Fertilize dates and timings suggested are for the central point of each geographical area listed. For the cooler Mountain areas, fertilize dates may be 1 to 2 weeks later in spring and 1 to 2 weeks earlier in fall; for warmer coastal regions, fertilizer dates may be 1 to 2 weeks earlier in spring and 1 to 2 weeks later in the fall than listed.

ing terms: "water-insoluble," "coated slow-release," "slow-release," "controlled release," "slowly available water soluble," or "occluded slow-release." Sulfur-coated urea is a source of water-insoluble nitrogen. Urea nitrogen is a water-soluble source of nitrogen.

Phosphorus

Phosphorous is another major element needed for plant growth and is the second number in a fertilizer analysis. Phosphorous is primarily involved in energy transformation within the plant. Phosphorous is generally required in smaller amounts than either nitrogen or potassium, and plays a critical role in the establishment of turfgrasses. On soils that are low in phosphorous, a light application of this element will increase the growth rate during establishment. High levels of phosphorous can cause problems with turfgrass growth. Centipedegrass is especially sensitive to high phosphorous levels so it is important to submit soil samples for nutrient analysis on a regular basis.

Potassium

Potassium is the third macroelement and the last number on a fertilizer analysis. This element is almost as important to turfgrass growth as nitrogen. Potassium is critical for plant growth from the establishment phase through complete coverage. Adequate levels of potassium in the soil will allow the plant to withstand environmental as well as mechanical stresses. In most turfgrasses sufficient potassium levels improve tolerance to heat, cold and drought. Also, diseases may become less of a problem.

For lawns, the best yearly fertilization program usually includes a combination of complete and nitrogen fertilizer applications. The **complete fertilizer** supplies nitrogen, phosphorus, and potassium, while the nitrogen material supplies mainly nitrogen. While nitrogen fertilization is based on the desired growth rate and type of turfgrass being grown, the phosphorus and potassium fertilization rate should be based on the recommendations of a soil test.

Both primary and secondary elements, if present, are listed on the fertilizer label. The label also tells the materials from which the fertilizer has been made. This information appears beside the "derived from" statement. An example of a **mixed fertilizer** containing several different sources of nitrogen is shown in Figure 12.

In addition to complete fertilizers, some materials are used almost exclusively to supply nitrogen

Figure 12

Example of a fertilizer label.

Lawn (Turf-Type) Fertilizer
16-4-8
Guaranteed Analysis

Total Nitrogen... 16%
   8.50% Ammoniacal Nitrogen
   2.00% Nitrate Nitrogen
   0.90% Water Soluble Organic Nitrogen
   4.60% **Water Insoluble Nitrogen**

Available Phosphoric Acid (P_2O_5)................... 4%

Soluble Potash (K_2O)..................................... 8%

---

to the lawn for rapid growth and dark green color. These materials include ammonium nitrate (33% N), ammonium sulfate (20% N), IBDU (31% N), urea (45% N), calcium nitrate (15.5% N), and ureaform (38% N).

Micronutrients

Fertilizers that contain micronutrients should be applied if a deficiency exists. This can be determined through tissue testing.

Many times warm-season grasses, such as centipedegrass, St. Augustinegrass, and zoysiagrass turn yellow in the spring due to a lack of nitrogen or iron. However, fertilizing with nitrogen may not be desirable, since it often encourages disease and insect problems. Often, the addition of iron to these grasses provides the desirable dark green color without stimulating excessive grass growth which often occurs when fertilizing with nitrogen. Usually iron sulfate (2 oz. per 3 to 5 gallons of water per 1,000 sq. ft.) or a chelated iron source are used to provide this greening effect. The effect from supplemental iron application is only temporary (about 2 to 4 weeks); therefore, repeat applications are necessary for summer-long color. Do not apply iron to wet grass or when the air temperatures is above 80 °F. Water-in immediately after application to minimize turf "burn" and to make the nutrients available to the grass plants.

Fertilizer Application Rate and Timing

Most fertilizers are applied at a rate determined by the type and amount of nitrogen present in the material. Nitrogen is the nutrient most used by the grass and often is the material that burns the lawn if applied at excessive rates. An almost universal rec-

ommendation for turfgrasses is to apply **1 lb. of actual nitrogen per 1,000 sq. ft. of lawn area if less than one-half (50%) of the nitrogen (N) is from a water-insoluble source.** If all of the nitrogen in the fertilizer is slow-release organic nitrogen, then the rate can be 2 lbs. of actual N per 1,000 sq. ft.

To determine how much fertilizer to apply to deliver 1 lb. of actual nitrogen, use this equation:

100÷% Nitrogen = amount of pounds of fertilizer required per 1,000 sq. ft. to apply 1 lb. of actual nitrogen.

For example, assume you have a 20-5-10 fertilizer that contains a quick-release, water-soluble nitrogen source such as ammonium sulfate. By using the formula (100 ÷ 20), you need to apply 5 lbs. of 20-5-10 per 1,000 sq. ft. of lawn to apply 1 lb. of actual nitrogen.

To apply $^1/_2$ pound of nitrogen per 1,000 square feet, use this equation:

50 ÷ % Nitrogen = amount of pounds of fertilizer required per 1,000 square feet to apply $^1/_2$ pound of actual nitrogen.

Table 8 lists a variety of fertilizers and their rate of application to apply 1 pound of N per 1,000 sq. ft.

Proper timing of nitrogen applications vary for cool- and warm-season turfgrasses because of their different growth cycles. Excessive spring application of nitrogen to cool-season turfgrasses is detrimental because it leads to excessive leaf growth at the expense of stored food reserves and root growth. This increases the injury to lawns from summer diseases and drought. Fall applications of nitrogen to warm-season lawns can predispose the grass to winter injury.

When a soil test of the lawn is not available, use Table 9 as a guide for fertilizing your lawn. Note that one program offers a "low maintenance" approach that will result in an average quality lawn. The "high maintenance" program is appropriate for those who seek an above-average quality lawn. The right schedule for you is the one that produces the quality of lawn you desire and fits your management style. For example, to obtain an average quality St. Augustinegrass lawn on the coast with a low maintenance program, apply a complete fertilizer (C) such as 16–4–8, 10–10–10, or 6–6–6 in April and August. Supplemental iron (Fe) applications can be made in June to provide green color without resulting in excessive lush grass growth.

Once you choose the appropriate fertilization schedule for your lawn, determine how much fertilizer you want to apply and how often. A range is suggested, but this amount could be higher or lower and frequency will be influenced depending on the quality of turf you desire, source of nitrogen, soil type, type and age of turfgrass, length of growing season, traffic, shade, and whether you recycle or return your clippings to the lawn.

Evaluate your lawn based on these factors because each one affects the amount and frequency of nitrogen application. Then, choose the amount and frequency that best suits your situation.

Quality Desired

Turfgrass quality is a measure of density, color, uniformity (free of weeds and off-type grasses), smoothness, growth habit, and texture. If you want an above-average quality lawn, you must make a commitment to selecting the right turfgrass species, mowing frequently, and applying slightly higher rates of nitrogen more often. In addition, irrigation, aerification, and pesticide applications may be necessary to enhance quality.

Soil Type

Sandy soils will generally leach more nitrogen than silt loam and clay loam soils. Therefore, more frequent nitrogen applications are often required in sandy soils when quick-release sources of nitrogen are used. Leaching can be minimized by using slow-release nitrogen sources, which in turn can reduce the possible contribution to the problem of nitrogen-enriched water in nearby streams and lakes.

To reduce the potential for runoff and to allow water to penetrate soil that is compacted, on slopes, or in natural drainage areas, you may need to aerate the soil. This is done by using a machine called an aerifier or core aerator, which pulls small cores of soil from the lawn.

Type and Age of Turfgrass

Nitrogen application to cool-season grasses, such as tall fescue is best done in late summer and fall. Warm-season grasses perform best when nitrogen is applied in mid-spring to midsummer. Newly established lawns or lawns lacking density or ground cover will benefit from properly timed applications of nitrogen until ground cover and density have reached a desirable level. A mature centipedegrass and carpetgrass lawn will require lower levels of nitrogen than other warm-season grasses.

Length of the Growing Season

A turfgrass growing in an area with a longer growing season will require more nitrogen.

Traffic

Where heavy traffic or use is anticipated, higher rates of properly timed nitrogen can help the grass recuperate and recover from injury.

Organic vs. Inorganic Fertilizers

There is much confusion over whether to use organic or inorganic fertilizers on lawns. Both types have advantages and disadvantages; the grass responds to both types. Grasses absorb nitrogen as nitrate or ammoniacal nitrogen. The nutrients in an organic fertilizer are contained in a complex system that is not readily dissolved in water and must be released through microbial activity. This means the fertilizer may be around for a long time if microbial activity is low, such as during the winter months. Organic nitrogen is not used directly by the plant, but must first be converted to the chemical form by soil microorganisms.

The advantages and disadvantages of inorganic fertilizers are outlined below:

Inorganic Nitrogen Sources

Advantages	Disadvantages
Quickly available N	Leach readily
Low cost per unit N	Danger of fertilizer burn
Easily controlled N levels	High salinity potential
Little problem of residual N	Must be applied frequently at low rates
Rapid plant response	Usually acid-forming

Organic Nitrogen Sources

Advantages	Disadvantages
Slow release of N	May be expensive
Less subject to leaching	Not readily released in cold weather
Small danger of lawn burn	Slow lawn response
Applied infrequently at high rates	May contain weed seeds (especially manures)

Shade

Grasses growing in heavily shaded areas require only $^1/_2$ to $^2/_3$ as much nitrogen as grasses growing in full sun. Reducing the amount of nitrogen to grasses growing in the shade reduces the incidence of disease. Since cool-season grass plants in shade can best use nitrogen when sunlight can reach the grass leaves, time your fertilizer application after the majority of leaves have fallen from the trees in the fall.

Clipping Recycling

A lawn receives significant amounts of nitrogen and potassium when clippings are returned. Recycling turfgrass clippings contributes very little to thatch and provides nutrients and organic matter.

Fertilizer Application Equipment

Fertilizers can be applied as either a dry or a liquid formulation. When applying a fertilizer, it is extremely important to apply it uniformly. Uneven fertilizer applications will result in an uneven greening or streaking in the lawn.

Excessive applications of a fertilizer may also "burn" the turf leaving brown or even dead areas. Fertilizer should be applied uniformly by using the right equipment applied at the correct rate with a properly calibrated spreader.

There are two basic types of dry fertilizer spreaders for use on the home lawn. The broadcast type, which is called a **rotary** or **cyclone spreader**, has a rotating disc that "throws out" fertilizer in a semicircular pattern as it is pushed (Figure 13). This type is best suited for covering large areas quickly. The distribution pattern is not uniform, but by controlling the overlap you can get good uniformity. Rotary spreaders usually give better distribution where sharp turns are encountered because they tend to cover a broader swath and fan the fertilizer out at the edges of the swath.

The **drop-type spreader** "drops" the fertilizer through a series of openings at the base of the hopper (Figure 14). This type is best suited for fertilizing small areas or when trying to prevent material from getting on sidewalks or paved surfaces. Drop-type spreaders are not as easy to maneuver around trees and shrubs as rotary spreaders. When using this kind of spreader, be sure to overlap the wheel tracks because all of the fertilizer is distributed between the wheels.

Each type of spreader has a dial to adjust the opening(s) or exit holes for the fertilizer. These opening settings vary for different kinds of fertilizers. Some companies list the settings of certain brand name spreaders on the fertilizer label. If your spreader is not listed, don't guess the appropriate setting. You should calibrate your spreader to determine the right setting that will dispense the correct amount of fertilizer. Calibration helps you avoid the mistake of applying too much, which can harm the lawn and the environment, or too little, and not achieve the results you expect.

Calibrating a Rotary Spreader

Follow these steps to calibrate a rotary or cyclone spreader.

Step 1. Gather the following materials:
- rotary spreader; check to see that the parts are in working order
- bucket
- hand-held calculator
- tape measure at least 50 ft. long
- scale for determining weight
- fertilizer

Step 2. A rotary spreader slings the fertilizer out in a wide, uneven pattern. More fertilizer falls in the center and less at the edges. About $^2/_3$ of the entire application width—called the "*effective width*"—receives a uniform amount of fertilizer. Therefore, you must measure the effective width of your spreader. Here's how:

    —Find a hard surface where you can measure the width of the fertilizer pattern.
    —Place a small amount of fertilizer into the spreader's hopper.

Figure 13

The rotating disk on a rotary spreader casts fertilizer out in a semicircular pattern.

—Walk a short distance at a regular pace and then stop.

—Measure the application width of the fertilizer band.

—Multiply the width by $^2/_3$ or 0.66.

For example, if the fertilizer is cast out in an 8 ft. wide swathe, the effective width is 5 ft. (0.66 x 8 ft.). This 5 ft. wide band receives an even amount of fertilizer. A 1 $^1/_2$ ft. wide band on either side receives less fertilizer.

—Sweep up the fertilizer and return it to the bag.

Knowing the effective width of your spreader makes the rest of the calibration process easier.

Step 3. When you're ready to fertilize your lawn, find a flat portion to calibrate the amount of delivered by your spreader. Mark off an area of your lawn that measures 1,000 sq. ft. In our example, the effective width is 5 ft. So, the length must be 200 ft. to create a 1,000 sq. ft. test area (1,000 sq. ft. ÷ 5 ft.).

Step 4. To apply 1 lb. of nitrogen per 1,000 sq. ft. with a 16-4-8 fertilizer, you need to spread 6 lbs. of fertilizer (100 ÷ 16). However, to deliver it uniformly to avoid any skips, make two passes. Apply one-half of the total amount in one direction and the other half at right angles to the first. So, calibrate the spreader based on one-half the application rate or 3 lbs. of 16-4-8 fertilizer.

Step 5. Weigh some fertilizer and put it in the hopper, say about 10 lbs., with the spreader in the "closed" position.

Step 6. Set your spreader according to the fertilizer label which may specify the setting for your spread-

er. If it's not listed, start at a low setting to avoid applying too much fertilizer.

Step 7. Start walking about 10 ft. behind the starting point you marked earlier. Open the spreader when you reach the starting line and are walking at a "normal" pace.

Step 8. Maintain a normal pace and close the hopper when you cross the finish.

Step 9. Weigh the remaining fertilizer in the spreader and subtract the final weight from the starting weight to determine how much fertilizer you applied over the 1,000 ft. area. For example, if you poured in 10 lbs. of fertilizer at the start and 8 lbs. was left over, then you spread 2 lbs. of fertilizer over the 1,000 sq. ft. area.

Step 10. At the setting you tested, you applied less nitrogen than you need. So, go back to step 5 and repeat the process with the spreader set at a higher setting. Move your calibration test site to another part of the lawn to avoid applying too much fertilizer to that area. Once you've found the correct setting that applies 3 lbs. of 16-4-8 per 1,000 sq. ft., record it for future reference.

Calibrating a Drop-type Spreader

Follow similar steps to calibrate a drop-type spreader.

Step 1. Check the spreader to make certain all parts are operating properly.

Step 2. Create a "catch pan" for the fertilizer. Make a V-shaped or box-shaped trough out of heavy cardboard or use a piece of aluminum guttering (Figure 15).

Step 3. Catch the fertilizer. Attach the trough se-

Figure 14

Drop-type spreader with calibration pan in foreground.

Figure 15

Drop-type spreader with calibration pan attached by string and quick-connect S-hooks.

curely beneath the spreader to catch the fertilizer.

Step 4. Measure the width of the spreader.

Step 5. Mark off an area that when multiplied by the width of the spreader will cover a 100 sq. ft. area. Divide 100 sq. ft. by the spreader width, or use the following table to help you determine how far you should walk to cover a 100 sq. ft. area:

Spreader Width	Travelling Distance
1.5 ft.	66.6 ft. (66 ft. 7 in.)
2 ft.	50 ft.
3 ft.	33.3 ft. (33 ft. 4 in.)

Step 6. Set the spreader on the opening number suggested by the manufacturer on the fertilizer bag. If there is no number, select the lowest setting and proceed at progressively higher settings (larger openings).

Step 7. Fill the spreader with fertilizer.

Step 8. Determine the amount of fertilizer that should be applied over the calibration area. For example, to apply 1 lb. of actual nitrogen per 1,000 sq. ft. using a 10-10-10 fertilizer, 10 lbs. of fertilizer will have to be applied per 1,000 sq. ft. (100 ÷ 10). Since the calibration area is only 100 sq. ft., only 1 lb. of fertilizer will have to be applied (100 sq. ft. divided by 10).

Step 9. Start walking. Open the spreader as you cross the starting line and walk the length of the calibration area. Close it at as you cross the finish line.

Step 10. Weigh the collected material and write it down next to the spreader settings. Take at least 3 trial runs for each setting. Then, average them to determine an average application rate for each particular setting.

Step 11. Select the right spreader setting. Assume you obtained the following results from your trials with your spreader:

Example of calibration trial results:

Setting	Average Output/100 sq. ft.
1	2 oz.
3	3 oz.
5	6 oz.
7	8 oz. ($\frac{1}{2}$ lb.)
9	10 oz.
11	16 oz. (1 lb.)

Use spreader setting 11 to apply 10 lbs. of 10-10-10 fertilizer per 1,000 sq. ft. (or 1 lb . of actual nitrogen per 1,000 sq. ft.). If you wanted to apply one-half of the total amount in one direction and the other half at 90° to the first to obtain uniform coverage, use spreader setting 7 to apply 5 lbs. of fertilizer per 1,000 sq. ft.

Use the same calibration procedure for any product you want to apply. Since the quantity applied depends on the physical properties of the material, the same settings cannot be used for different materials, even if the ratios are the same. Once the spreader is calibrated and set for the proper rate, any size area can be treated accurately.

Mowing

Mowing is one of the primary maintenance practices essential for producing a good quality lawn. Mowing is the process that creates a lawn, rather than a pasture or meadow. It directly affects the health and quality of a lawn. When mowing a lawn, important factors to consider include height of cut, frequency of cut, and the type of mower used. For the best appearance, turfgrasses should be mowed at their ideal height as determined by the grass species. A grass that spreads horizontally can usually be mowed shorter than an upright-growing bunch-type grass. Grasses with narrow blades can generally be mowed closer than grasses with wide blades. Turfgrasses under stress, such as heat, drought, or shade should be mowed at a higher height of cut. Table 10 outlines suggested mowing heights for lawn turfgrasses in South Carolina.

Proper mowing is important in creating a good quality lawn because it encourages a dense stand of grass plants. A dense turf keeps out weeds through competition for sunlight and nutrients. A weak, thin turf allows weed seeds to germinate and grow.

Frequency of Cut

Mow your lawn regularly. A good rule-of-thumb is to remove no more than one-third of the grass height at any one mowing. For example, if you are maintaining your centipede lawn at $1\frac{1}{2}$ inches, mow the lawn when it is about 2 inches high. Cutting off more than one-third at one time can stop the roots from growing and would require frequent watering during dry summers to keep the plants alive. Also, following the one-third rule will produce smaller clippings which will disappear quickly by filtering down to the soil surface. If the grass becomes too tall between mowings, raise the mowing height and then gradually reduce it until the recommended height is reached.

Fertilize with Caution

All fertilizers may burn if improperly applied. Never exceed the recommended rate or the lawn may be damaged. Always apply fertilizers when the grass leaves are dry and water thoroughly after application to wash the fertilizer into the soil where the nutrients can be used by the grass plants. This will also reduce the potential for surface runoff, especially on slopes, and volatilization.

Avoid applying fertilizer to nonturfed or impervious areas (driveways, roads, or bare soil. Also, avoid fertilizing close to the shoreline of streams, rivers, and lakes. Install a non-mowed, vegetated buffer strip to absorb any nutrients to prevent them from contaminating the water.

Never leave unused fertilizer in the hopper. Fertilizer salts are corrosive and could ruin the spreader. Be sure to collect the unused fertilizer and pour it back into the bag, not on the driveway or road. The spreader should be rinsed thoroughly with water and allowed to dry. Lubricate the spreader with a light machine oil to prevent rusting and to keep the working parts in good condition.

Type of Mowers Used

Lawn mowers are available in a wide variety of sizes and styles with a variety of features. Two basic types of mowers are **rotary mowers** (Figure 16) and **reel mowers** (Figure 17). More recently, mulching, flail, and string mowers have been introduced. Most mowers can be obtained as push- or self-propelled models. Front, side, and rear clipping discharge models are available. The choice of mower often depends on personal preference. Points to consider when purchasing a mower are the size of the lawn, turfgrass species, and level of lawn maintenance.

Rotary mowers are the most popular because of their low cost, easy maneuverability, and simple maintenance. The mower blade cuts the grass blade on impact. Most rotary mowers cannot give a quality cut lower than one inch; however, they are versatile and can be used on taller grasses and weeds, for mulching grass clippings, and for general trimming.

A modification of rotary mowers is **mulching mowers**. These are designed to cut leaf blades into very small pieces that are able to fall into the lawn rather than remain on top of the grass. Being so small, these pieces can decompose quicker than blades cut to traditional size. The mower blades are designed to create a mild vacuum in the mower deck until the leaf blades are cut into these small pieces. Mulching mowers do not have the traditional discharge chute as do most rotary mowers. Refer to Table 11 for a list of the advantages and disadvantages of mulching mowers.

Table 10

Suggested mowing heights for cool- and warm-season turfgrasses.

Turfgrass	Cutting Height (inches)	Frequency (days)	Best Mower Type
Kentucky bluegrass*	$1\frac{1}{2}$ to $2\frac{1}{2}$	7 to 14	Rotary
Fine fescue	2 to 3	10 to 14	Rotary
Tall fescue*	$2\frac{1}{2}$ to $3\frac{1}{2}$	7 to 14	Rotary
Ryegrass (overseeding)	$1\frac{1}{2}$ to $2\frac{1}{2}$	7 to 14	Rotary
Bahiagrass	3 to 4	7 to 17	Rotary or flail
Bermudagrass			
--Common	1 to $1\frac{1}{2}$	3 to 5	Reel or rotary
--Hybrid	$\frac{3}{4}$ to $1\frac{1}{4}$	3 to 5	Reel
Carpetgrass	1 to 2	10 to 14	Rotary
Centipedegrass	1 to 2	10 to 14	Rotary
St. Augustinegrass			
--regular varieties	$2\frac{1}{2}$ to 4	7 to 14	Rotary
--semidwarf	$1\frac{1}{2}$ to $2\frac{1}{2}$	7 to 14	Rotary
Zoysiagrass	$\frac{3}{4}$ to $1\frac{1}{2}$	10 to 14	Reel

*Only certain varieties will tolerate the lower mowing heights.

Figure 16

Adjusting the height of a rotary mower on a level surface.

Figure 17

A reel mower is well-suited for mowing hybrid bermudagrasses and zoysiagrasses.

Reel mowers are for highly maintained lawns where appearance is important. Reel mowers cut with a scissor-like action to produce a very clean, even cut. They are used at cutting heights of two inches or less. Bermudagrass and zoysiagrass are best cut with a reel mower. Reel-type mowers require a relatively smooth surface to obtain a quality cut. Using reel mowers on extremely uneven surfaces will result in scalped areas.

The number of blades needed to produce a smooth uniform cut depends on the mowing height. Generally, as the height is lowered, the greater the number of blades is required on the reel (Table 12).

Maintaining a sharp cutting blades, which cut the grass cleanly, ensuring rapid healing and re-growth. When dull blades tear and bruise the leaves, the wounded grass plants become weakened and are less able to ward off invading weeds or to recover from disease and insect attacks.

Table 11

Advantages and disadvantages of mulching mowers.

Advantages
1. Clippings are returned to the lawn, which recycles nutrients back to the turf.
2. Mulching eliminates the effort of collecting clippings.

Disadvantages
1. Mulching mowers are ineffective on wet or tall grass.
2. Blades must be kept sharp.
3. Current models are small and require high horsepower engines.

Table 12

The number of blades needed on a reel mower for various cutting heights.

Cutting height	Number of blades
> 1 inch	5
$1/2$ to 1 inch	6
$1/4$ to $1/2$ inch	7 to 9
< $1/4$ inch	11 to 13

Return or recycle your grass clippings to the lawn. Grass clippings contain about 4% nitrogen, $1/2$ to 1% phosphorus, 2 to 3% potassium, and smaller amounts of other essential plant nutrients—basically a 4-1-3 fertilizer. When left on the lawn, these nutrients are eventually returned to the soil.

String mowers are similar to rotary mowers, but the blade has been replaced with a monofilament line. This is a definite safety feature when operating the mower in some locations. A high speed motor is needed in these mowers to spin the line fast enough for a clean cut. String mowers are most often used for trimming, edging, and cutting hard-to-mow areas.

Don't Bag It!
Grass clippings *do not* contribute to thatch in any lawn. Thatch is a layer of living and dead plant parts that lies between the grass leaves and the soil surface. The plant tissue that makes up thatch contains a high amount of hard-to-decompose cell wall material called lignin. Grass leaves mostly comprise water (75 to 85% by weight), high amounts of protein, and little lignin. The clippings break down quickly once they fall down between the grass blades and onto the soil surface.

Additional Lawn Maintenance Practices

Irrigating

Turfgrasses, like all living plants, require water for growth and survival. Since rainfall patterns vary, seasonal droughts are common in South Carolina. During long, dry hot periods in the summer, you have two choices when it comes to lawn irrigation: (1) do not water and allow the lawn to turn brown and go dormant or (2) water the grass to keep it green. Unfortunately, each choice bears some consequences. Besides increasing mowing time, watering may encourage weed growth, stimulate disease outbreaks, and raise your water bill.

Some turfgrass species and cultivars have the ability to survive dry periods better than others. The most **drought resistant** warm-season grasses are bahiagrass, common and hybrid bermudagrasses, and zoysiagrass (Table 13). Under severe drought conditions with no supplemental irrigation, these turfgrasses go dormant and turn brown as growth ceases and the leaves die. When favorable moisture conditions return, new growth emerges from buds in their crowns, rhizomes, and stolons. Deep root systems also help turfgrasses recuperate from dry spells.

Tall fescue will go dormant and turn brown during moderate summer drought periods; however, it quickly recovers with rain. On the other hand, severe summertime drought conditions with no wa-

Table 13

Relative drought resistance of turfgrasses (listed alphabetically within each category).

Relative Drought Resistance	Turfgrass
Excellent	Bahiagrass
	Common bermudagrass
	Zoysiagrass
Very good	Hybrid bermudagrass
	St. Augustinegrass
Good	Centipedegrass
	Fine fescue
	Ky. bluegrass
	Seashore paspalum
	Tall fescue
Fair	Perennial ryegrass
Poor	Carpetgrass

ter for three weeks or more often result in thinned-out fescue lawns that have to be reseeded in the fall.

If You Water...Decide When to Water

The most efficient way to water a lawn is to apply water when the lawn begins to show signs of stress from lack of water. Use the following techniques to identify signs or indications of water need:

Color test

When water becomes unavailable for an extended period, a lawn will exhibit a bluish-gray cast.

Good Mowing Practices

- Pick up all stones, sticks, and other debris before mowing to avoid damaging the mower or injuring someone with flying objects.
- Never mow wet turf with a rotary mower because clippings can clog the machine. Mow only when the turf is dry.
- Sharpen the mower blade frequently enough to prevent a ragged appearance to the turf.
- Mow in a different direction every time the lawn is cut. This helps prevent wear patterns, reduces the "grain" (grass laying over in the same direction), and reduces the possibility of scalping.
- Do not remove clippings. If clumping occurs, distribute these by mowing over them or by lightly raking them.
- Check your mower every time it is used.
- Follow manufacturer's recommendations for service and adjustments.
- Adjust the cutting height by setting the mower on a level driveway or sidewalk and using a ruler to measure the distance between the ground and the blade.
- Never fill a hot mower with gasoline.
- Always wear heavy leather shoes when mowing the lawn.
- Wash the mower after using it to reduce rusting and weed seed movement.

Footprinting

Walk across your lawn late in the day and examine the lawn behind you to see if your steps left any "footprints." Your footprints will appear in a lawn when the grass plants have low levels of water in their tissues. When the grass blades are compressed by your feet, the low water levels prevent the grass blades from springing back up. If your footprints remain for an extended period of time, the lawn should be watered to prevent the grass from turning brown and becoming dormant.

Leaf check

During dry periods, grass leaves respond by wilting, rolling, or folding, similar to corn. Use these symptoms as a signal that watering is necessary to prevent the turfgrass from becoming dormant.

Screwdriver test

Press a screwdriver (or a reasonable facsimile) into the lawn. If the soil is very dry, it will be difficult to push the screwdriver into the ground. Use the screwdriver test to confirm the results of the other visual methods to help judge when you should water your lawn.

Amount of Water to Apply

The amount of water to apply at any one time varies with the amount of water present in the soil, the water-holding capacity of the soil, and drainage characteristics. Efficient watering wets only the turfgrass rootzone, does not saturate the soil, and does not allow water to run off.

When the soil is dry, then $3/_4$ to 1 inch of water is required to wet the area thoroughly. This is equivalent to 465 to 620 gallons of water for each 1,000 sq. ft. of lawn.

Generally, turfgrasses require no more than 0.3 inches of water per day (Table 14). Under extreme summer conditions, water use can be as high as 0.4 inches of water per day. During the winter when grasses are not actively growing, water use can be as little as 0.05 inches of water per day.

A simple watering schedule would be to apply $3/_4$ inch of water when the lawn shows water deficiency symptoms as discussed earlier. This amount of water, which will replace the water lost by the lawn grasses during summer dry spells, will moisten the root zone area. Once you apply this amount, do not apply any more until water stress symptoms reappear.

Table 14

General average summer turfgrass evapotranspiration (ET)* rates in humid regions. Generally, ET rates at other seasons are much lower.

Turfgrass	Summer ET Rates	
	in/day	in/week
Bahiagrass	0.25	1.75
Bermudagrass	0.12	0.84
Centipedegrass	0.15	1.05
Ky. bluegrass	0.15	1.05
Perennial ryegrass	0.15	1.05
Seashore paspalum	0.25	1.75
St. Augustinegrass	0.13	0.91
Tall fescue	0.15	1.05
Zoysiagrass	0.14	0.98

*The combined loss of water by evaporation from the soil and transpiration from the leaves.

If you have a heavy clay soil and cannot apply all of this amount at once due to water running off from the lawn, apply a little at a time and allow the water to soak in before you continue. Determine the depth of penetration with the "screwdriver test." If you have a portable sprinkler, move it frequently to avoid surface runoff and excessive water use.

Typically, two to three waterings per week in the summer and once every 10 to 14 days in the winter are required. If rainfall occurs, adjust the irrigation rate according to the amount of rainfall you received.

Water should never be applied at a rate faster than it can be absorbed by the soil. If the sprinkler applies too much water, it runs off and is wasted. This seldom happens with small sprinklers unless the lawn is very dense or the soil is compacted.

Manner of Applying Water

Water should never be applied at a rate faster than it can be absorbed by the soil. If the sprinkler applies too much water, it runs off and is wasted. This seldom happens with small sprinklers, unless the lawn is thick or the soil is compacted.

Avoid extremes in watering frequency and amount. Light, frequent watering is inefficient and encourages shallow root systems. Excessive irrigation, which keeps the root system saturated with water, is harmful to the lawn and encourages pests such as weeds and diseases. Roots need a balance of water and air to function and grow properly.

The time of watering is important. Water late in the evening after dewfall or early in the morning: these are the most efficient and beneficial times. Water evaporation is minimized so that a high proportion of the applied water is used by the grass plants. Also, early morning irrigation may curtail the development and spread of diseases. Grass blades dry off quickly, reducing the probability of fungus spores from germinating and infecting the leaf tissues. Watering in late afternoon or late morning may be detrimental if it extends the time the lawn is naturally wet from dew. However, you may have no control over when you can water if you use municipal water, since you may have to schedule your watering to avoid peak residential water use.

Once you water, do not water again until you observe symptoms of water deficiency. Avoid watering grass every day except during the establishment of newly seeded, sodded, or sprigged lawns. Otherwise, watering every day with a small amount will encourage shallow rooting, making the grass less drought-tolerant. Try to stretch the interval between waterings to as many days as possible to encourage the development of a deep, extensive root system.

Once you choose to water your lawn during the summer months, continue watering. Encouraging the lawn to break dormancy and then not watering again will exhaust the plant, resulting in injury or death.

Calibrating Your Sprinkler System

To water efficiently, you need to know how much water your irrigation system applies over a certain time period. Most people irrigate their lawn for a given number of minutes without knowing how much water they are applying. This leads either to watering too little or too much. Excess water either runs down sidewalks and streets or through the root zone and deep below ground out-of-reach of turfgrass roots.

Calibrating or determining the rate of water your sprinkler system applies is an easy job. Use the following step-by-step procedure if you have an in-ground system or a sprinkler at the end of a hose.

Step 1. Obtain several (5 to 10) coffee cans, tuna fish cans, or other straight-sided containers to catch the irrigation water. Use identical containers that are about 3 to 6 inches in diameter.

Step 2. If you have an in-ground system, place the containers in one zone at a time. Randomly scatter the cans within the zone. Repeat the entire procedure in every zone because the irrigation rates may differ. If you use a hose-end sprinkler to water your lawn, place the containers in a straight line from the sprinkler to the edge of the watering pattern. Space the containers evenly apart.

Step 3. Turn the water on for 15 minutes.

Water-saving Ideas
Here are some pointers to help you save water this summer when watering your lawn:
- Let the lawn "show" you when it needs water. Look at your footprints, a bluish-green or bluish-gray cast, or folded or wilted leaves.
- You do not have to water the entire lawn. Consider only those areas that need water. Identify highly drought-prone areas: high spots, sandy locations, and areas adjacent to sidewalks, patios, and driveways.
- Apply no more than $3/4$ to 1 inch of water when you irrigate once each week.
- Do not water when rain is forecast in your area.
- In lawns comprised of compacted clay soil where water does not penetrate easily, aerate the lawn. Loosen up the soil with a spading fork or use a powered machine that creates holes or "pores" in the lawn by the action of spoons or tines mounted on a drum or reel. As the machine rolls over the lawn, it removes cores of soil from the ground, loosening the soil. The holes also serve as water reservoirs by collecting water which reduces surface runoff. Cool-season lawns are best aerated in the fall while warm-season lawns should be aerated in the summer.
- If you have an in-ground, automatic sprinkler system, set the time clock to "off" and manually turn the system "on" when the lawn needs water. The automatic position on the time clock is useful when you are away from home for more than a few days. Even then, the clock can be made to operate more efficiently by installing a rain shut-off device which overrides the system when it rains.
- Fix leaky hoses, spigots, and valves. A considerable amount of water is wasted with leaky hose connections and worn-out spigots. Also, check sprinkler heads for an even spray pattern and direction of spray; check for damaged sprinkler heads and replace heads that leak.

Step 4. After the elapsed time, collect the cans and pour the water into a single can.

Step 5. Measure the depth of water you collected during the 15-minute period.

Step 6. Calculate the average depth of water by dividing the amount of collected water in inches by the number of cans.

Step 7. Multiply the average depth by 4 to determine the application rate in inches per hour.

Now that you know your sprinkler system irrigation rate, you can more efficiently apply water to your turf.

Use Table 15 as a guide for sprinkler times. For example, if the sprinkler system applies water at the rate of 2 inches per hour and you want to apply $1/2$ inch, then run the sprinklers for 15 minutes. To determine how long to run a sprinkler system for irrigation rates not listed in the table, use the following equation:

$$\text{Minutes required to run each zone} = \frac{\text{Amount of water to be applied} \times 60}{\text{Your calibrated irrigation rate}}$$

Table 15
Time required to apply water for a given irrigation rate.

Amount water to be applied	Irrigation Rate (Amount of water per hour)			
	$1/2$ in.	1 in.	$1^1/_2$ in.	2 in.
	Minutes to run each zone			
$1/4$ in.	30	15	10	8
$1/2$ in.	60	30	20	15
$3/4$ in.	90	45	30	23
1 in.	120	60	40	30

Calibration Pointers
- Try to calibrate the sprinkler system during the same time the system is normally run so that water pressures are similar.
- Low water pressure can significantly reduce the amount and coverage of water applied by a sprinkler system.
- Never apply more than 1 inch of water per irrigation. Stop watering if water is running off.
- Most time clocks can be adjusted for accurate time settings. Consult a local sprinkler company for details.
- If you use a hose-end sprinkler, a mechanical time and shut-off switch that attaches to the faucet will help make watering more efficient.
- Avoid mixing sprinkler head types. Mist heads apply more water than impact heads. Match sprinkler heads for uniform coverage.
- Check the sprinkler system frequently. Replace broken sprinkler heads, clear clogged nozzles, and adjust the spray direction.

Aerifying

The practice of physically removing cores of soil and leaving holes or cavities in the lawn is called **core aeration** or **aerification**. Aerifying has the following benefits:

- Loosens compacted soil and increases the availability of water and nutrients.
- Enhances oxygen levels in the soil, stimulating root growth and enhancing the activity of thatch-decomposing organisms.
- While removing cores of soil, the spoons or tines also sever roots, rhizomes, and stolons. Grass plants are stimulated to produce new shoots and roots which "fill up" the holes in the lawn and increase the density of the turf.
- Reduces water runoff.
- Increases the lawn's drought tolerance and improves its overall health.

Aerification of home lawns is generally used to correct soil problems and is not used as a routine practice.

Cool-season lawns are best aerified in the fall when there is less danger of invasion by weedy annuals. Allow at least 4 weeks of good growing weather to help the plants recover. Warm-season lawns are best aerified in late spring and summer when they are actively growing. Ideally, the soil should be moderately moist, which makes the soil easier to penetrate.

To aerify large lawn areas, professionals use a power-driven core aerator or aerifier. The working parts of these machines are spoon-shaped tines or hollow tubes (Figure 18). As the tubes are driven into the lawn, cores of soil are removed from the ground and strewn across the lawn. Both types of tines work equally well, but the hollow tine makes a somewhat cleaner hole than the spoon type and brings up less soil. The tine size varies up to $3/4$

Figure 18

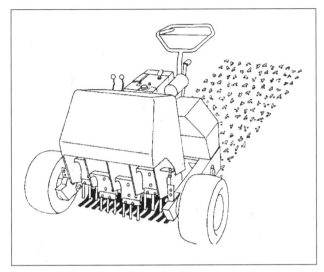

Core aerification improves soil aeration, which enhances the movement of air and water into the soil.

inch in diameter and penetrates up to 3 inches in depth, depending on the manufacturer's specifications. The closer tine placement removes more soil, exposes more soil surface area for water and fertilizer movement, and alleviates compaction quicker than the wider tine spacing.

Penetration depth depends on soil type, soil moisture, tine diameter, and the weight and power of the aerifier. Soil cores should be left on the lawn to be broken up by rainfall and traffic. If their appearance bothers you, you can speed up their disappearance by raking them into the grass. Whichever machine you use, go over the lawn at least twice: first in one direction and then second in a perpendicular direction.

Aerification can be combined with seeding, particularly on sparse or bare areas. If you are going to seed the lawn, make 6 to 10 passes over the area with a machine. You need to produce a number of holes, at least 4 inches apart, to improve the appearance and density of the stand. Allow the holes to heal about a month before seeding. If you overseed immediately after coring, seeds that land in or near the aerifier holes will germinate and grow much better than those between the holes, giving the lawn an uneven appearance. With a fraction of the effort and expense of tilling up the entire area, combining aerification with seeding will give the lawn a brand-new look.

Dethatching

Thatch is a dense, spongy collection of living and dead grass stems and roots lying between the soil surface and green grass leaves in established lawns (Figure 19). There is a gradual decrease in size of organic matter from the top of the thatch layer to the bottom of the mat. **Mat** is very fine, dense, and peat-like, and is not very compressible.

Thatch originates from old stems, stolons (above-ground stems), roots, and rhizomes (below-ground stems) shed by grasses during the development of new plant parts. The sloughed-off plant matter collects at the soil surface and gradually decomposes. Grass leaves or clippings decay rapidly because they have the lowest amount of lignin in their tissues and decay rapidly. However, stems, stolons, rhizomes, and roots decompose slowly, in part, because of the high levels of lignin present in their tissues. When the accumulation rate of plant litter exceeds the decomposition rate, a thatch layer develops.

Reducing Summertime Stress

Follow these steps to help your lawn deal with the stresses of summer weather:

- Test your soil and follow a fertilization program according to the soil test results. Add the appropriate amount of lime or sulfur and maintain adequate levels of phosphorus and potassium to encourage deep rooting and drought resistance.
- Reduce thatch layers thicker than $\frac{1}{2}$ inch by dethatching. Heavy thatch layers may contain more grass roots than soil, thus making the grass plants less tolerant to drought and more susceptible to heat injury.
- Use natural fertilizers with "slowly available" or "insoluble" nitrogen and synthetic fertilizers that contain slow-release nitrogen, such as urea formaldehyde or sulfur-coated urea. The nitrogen in these types of fertilizer does not quickly wash away and provides green color without causing excessive leaf growth.
- Raise the mowing height of your lawn mower during the summer months: a higher mowing height encourages root growth and reduces heat stress.

Thatch is not omnipresent because lawn grasses differ in their propensity to produce thatch. Tall fescue, perennial ryegrass, bahiagrass, and centipedegrass also form thatch, but at a slower rate in contrast to other kinds of grasses. Highly vigorous cultivars or turfgrass species which experience quick growth rates, such as Kentucky bluegrass and hybrid bermudagrass cultivars, are heavy thatch-builders. Slower-growing grasses, such as red fescue and zoysiagrass, also produce thatch because their fibrous tissues are highly resistant to decomposition which collect on the soil surface.

Figure 19

Cross-section of St. Augustinegrass lawn illustrating a thatch layer.

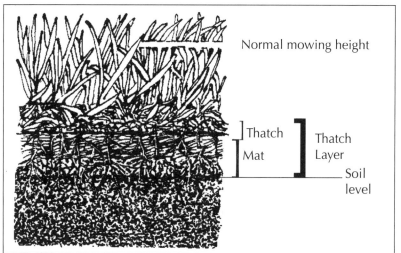

Normal mowing height

Thatch Mat

Thatch Layer

Soil level

Disadvantages of Thatch

If the thatch layer is more than $1/2$ inch thick, the disadvantages outweigh the advantages. In heavily thatched lawns, grass plants tend to grow within this thatch layer. Their roots rely on the thatch for nutrients and moisture, but thatch retains neither well. Any fertilizer applied to the lawn will not be absorbed by the grass and will be lost to the soil where few, if any, grass roots reside.

Watering becomes a problem on heavily thatched lawns. Thatch dries out easily and re-wets with difficulty. Eventually isolated dry spots develop. The lawn becomes less drought-tolerant and becomes more susceptible to heat injury, wilting, and drying out. A "Catch-22" situation arises: the lawn needs to be irrigated frequently to keep it alive, but watering repeatedly causes the nutrients to leach out of the thatch and into the soil which contains few grass roots.

While a thick thatch layer hinders grass growth, it provides a safe haven for insects and diseases. Thatch acts like an "organic" barrier which blocks the movement of pesticides and reduces their effectiveness. Hence, thatchy lawns are plagued with pest problems.

Reducing Thatch Buildup

A thatch layer signals an imbalance between decomposition and accumulation of plant litter. To speed up decomposition, maintain an environment that encourages the proliferation of thatch-decomposing keep it at the recommended level. Acidic soils hamper the activity of earthworms, insects, and microbes involved in thatch decomposition.

Highly compacted soils or finely textured soils, particularly heavy clay soils, impair the activity of soilborne organisms due to restricted oxygen levels. Periodic core aerification or coring will alleviate compaction and will facilitate the movement of air and water into the soil. Coring is a cultural practice which will not remove substantial amounts of thatch but will improve the soil environment to benefit lawn grasses and the earthworms and microbes engaged in breaking down thatch. If you use pesticides, use them sparingly and locally to control specific pest problems. Judicious pesticide use can minimize the destruction of thatch-decomposers in the lawn.

Thatch accumulation can be controlled by applying appropriate levels of nitrogen and water to meet the needs of the lawn. Lavish amounts of nitrogen and water produce an excessive amount of succulent growth which increases thatch and often makes the lawn more susceptible to pests.

Mow at the proper height and mow frequently. Reduce the height of the lawn by removing no more than one-third of the grass height at any one mowing. Excessive thatch layers may accumulate by mowing infrequently or cutting at high heights, particularly on warm-season grasses like bermuda and zoysiagrass. The use of a mulching mower alone will not prevent a thatch problem.

Thatch Removal

Examine the depth of the thatch layer by cutting out a pie-shaped wedge of sod from the lawn with a knife or spade. If the layer is thicker than $^1/_2$ inch, you need to dethatch or physically remove it from the lawn. Remember that a thatch buildup is gradual and occurs over a period of years; therefore, a thatch removal program should also be gradual.

For a small area, consider using a dethatching rake. As you pull the rake across the lawn, the sharp curved blades slide through the thatch and lift it from the lawn.

A large area requires power-driven dethatching equipment and know-how. Improper dethatching can devastate a lawn. If you'd prefer to dethatch the lawn rather than hire a reputable commercial lawn maintenance company, choose the most effective dethatcher available: a **vertical mower** (Figure 20). Select a vertical mower with revolving, straight fixed blades; the spacing between the knives and depth should be adjustable. Vary the spacing of the blades according to the kind of grass in the lawn.

For the cool-season grasses, Kentucky bluegrass and red fescue, the blades should be spaced 1 to 2 inches apart. For warm-season grasses, space blades 1 to 2 inches apart for bermudagrass and zoysiagrass, 2 to 3 inches for centipede, and 3 inches for St. Augustinegrass. The blades should cut into the thatch layer and at least $^1/_2$ inch into the soil. You should

expect the vertical mower to lift thatch to the surface and cultivate the soil without causing serious injury to the grass plants. The blades cut into the thatch layer and lift it to the surface where it can be raked up and added to the compost pile or used as a mulch in the vegetable garden.

Lawns containing grasses with rhizomes, such as Kentucky bluegrass and zoysiagrass, may be vertically mowed in several directions without killing the lawn. However, grasses with stolons, such as centipedegrass and St. Augustinegrass, may be killed with multiple passes. They should only be vertically mowed in one direction to avoid removing too much plant material and reducing the rate of recovery.

If the thatch layer exceeds 2 to 3 inches, widen the spacing of the blades to reduce injury to the grass plants and remove only a portion of the thatch layer at a time. Allow the lawn to fully recover before you attempt to reduce the depth of the layer any further.

The best time to remove thatch is in late summer or early fall for cool-season lawns. Dethatch warm-season grasses in spring after greenup or in early summer when the grass is growing rapidly and the weather is not so hot that the lawn is under drought stress. Since vertical mowing is a traumatic experience for the lawn, plan to dethatch with a cushion of at least a month of favorable growing conditions and avoid excessively hot or dry periods.

After dethatching, rake or sweep up the dead material and add it to the compost pile or use it as a mulch in the vegetable garden. Thoroughly water the lawn to prevent the exposed roots from drying

Figure 20

A vertical mower uses blades to cut and lift the thatch from the lawn.

out. About a week after dethatching, apply 1 lb. of actual nitrogen (<50% quick-release, water-soluble nitrogen) per 1,000 sq. ft. of lawn and irrigate afterwards to minimize burn. Follow a good lawn management program that includes preventive practices to reduce thatch accumulation and curative practices to remove the excess.

Power raking uses the same mechanical principles as vertical mowing. This specialized machine uses evenly spaced, flexible spring steel tines that revolve at high speed to strip through turf and loosen debris for subsequent removal. The machine and procedures are often confused with vertical mowing. Power raking does not involve a cutting action, as does vertical mowing. Therefore, it is not a substitute for vertical mowing and thatch removal.

Close mowing is a procedure where the turf is mowed to a much shorter height than normal. It is a poor substitute for vertical mowing, but its use, especially in early spring, at or just before new growth begins to appear, may delay the need for vertical mowing where a shallow thatch layer exists. The mowing height will vary with turfgrass species. Turfgrasses with rhizomes, like bermudagrass and zoysiagrass, may be mowed closely near the soil surface. Centipedegrass and St. Augustinegrass spread by above-ground runners called stolons. Removing these stolons would kill the turf. Zoysiagrass is not as sensitive to close mowing as centipede and St. Augustine, but it is more sensitive than bermuda. Mowing below the crown or green growing points of zoysia will cause extensive damage. After mowing, collect and compost the dead plant material.

Topdressing

Topdressing with sand is a somewhat lost practice that provides numerous benefits. Most notable is thatch decomposition, covering of stolons, and smoothing the turf surface. Sand is the most commonly used topdressing material. It should be weed-free and not contain excessive silt and clay. If river bottom sand is used, have it washed to remove these. Topdressing is best for centipedegrass, bermudagrass and zoysiagrass. It is performed on these grasses in late spring or summer, typically applying ¼- to ½-inch-thick layers. Following topdressing, the sand should be incorporated by either brushing it in or dragging a piece of carpet across it.

Integrated Pest Management

IPM is basically common-sense pest control. IPM involves the use of three different pest control tactics—cultural, biological, and chemical—to get the best long-term results with the least disruption to the environment.

A cultural control approach for managing pests includes the following components:

1. **Pest-resistant plants.** One of the oldest means of pest control has been through careful breeding and selection of resistant or tolerant plants. For example, Floratam and FX-10 St. Augustinegrasses are noted for their resistance to chinch bugs.

2. **Pest-free seed, sods, and sprigs.** SC has a certification program to provide pest-free propagation material. Each bag of certified seed must provide information on purity and germination percentages. In addition, a weed seed listing must be provided, and no noxious weed seeds are allowed. When planting sprigs or sod, inspect the turf for weeds, fire ants, and other pests. These steps will help to prevent or reduce pest problems during and after establishment.

3. **Good site preparation.** Properly preparing a planting site is an important step in pest management, primarily due to its effects on the health and resilience of the turf.

4. **Proper lawn care.** Probably the best defense against pest invasion is by maintaining a dense, healthy, competitive turf. This is achieved by providing cultural practices that favor turf growth. Important cultural practices in IPM programs include proper watering, fertilization, mowing, aerification, at the recommended height to shade out weeds, watering and fertilizing properly, and controlling thatch.

A biological pest control tactic relies on natural enemies of the pests, which may be parasites and predators. A popular biological control approach to managing Japanese beetle grubs is with milky disease, a naturally occurring bacteria (*Bacillus popilliae*) that primarily infects Japanese beetle grubs. When the Japanese beetle grubs become infected with milky disease, they eventually die, releasing billions of spores into the soil to infect future generations of grubs. Unfortunately, variable success has resulted in the use of this biological control.

Chemical control, the final component of an IPM approach, involves the judicious use of pesti-

To reduce the accumulation of thatch, follow these practices:
- Fertilize according to soil test recommendations and be sure to avoid applying excessive amounts of nitrogen.
- Mow your lawn at the proper height and frequency.
- Aerify your lawn in late spring and summer with a machine that creates "pores" in the lawn by the action of spoons or tines mounted on a drum or reel. As the machine rolls over the lawn, it removes cores of soil from the ground. The earthen cores or plugs are deposited on the lawn and contain microorganisms that help to break down the thatch.
- Monitor the soil pH and keep it at the recommended level for your particular turfgrass. Acidic soils hamper the activity of earthworms, insects, and microbes involved in breaking down thatch.

cides. Before using a pesticide in an IPM program, you need to make a few decisions:

1. **Identify the pest.** Determine if the pest population and level of damage is sufficient to warrant the use of a pesticide.
2. **Treat the pest when it is most susceptible and the lawngrasses are most tolerant.** Best control of many insects and weeds occurs at a particular stage in its life cycle, which is usually during the early stages of development. For example, mole crickets are most susceptible to chemical control when they are small, usually during the months of May or June. Chemical applications at other times are less effective.
3. **If you need to use a pesticide, select one that is most effective, but least toxic to nontarget organisms and least persistent in the environment.** Read the label completely and thoroughly. Determine the size of the affected area and treat only those locations. Spot-treat, if possible, instead of making "blanket" applications.

Weed Management

Weeds are considered "pests" in most home lawns because they differ in color, leaf size, shape, and growth habit from desirable turfgrasses. Also, weeds compete with turfgrasses for sunlight, soil moisture, and plant nutrients. A properly managed lawn should crowd out most weeds. For an above-average quality lawn with a minimum number of

grassy and broadleaf weeds, some form of weed control may be necessary.

Development of Weed Problems

Most turfgrass weeds develop from seeds that were present, but inactive, in the soil. Some weeds develop from seeds introduced in contaminated topsoil, manure, compost, mulch, turfgrass seed or sod. Still others develop from seeds carried into an area by wind, equipment or animals. Regardless of their origin, thousands of seeds may be present in the soil.

Weed Establishment and Competition

In a healthy, dense stand of turf, little light reaches the soil surface. Any weed seedlings that do emerge from the soil surface are short-lived because their leaves do not receive enough light for photosynthesis. However, if the lawn is thin or bare, and favorable light, moisture and temperature conditions exist, weed seeds germinate and they become established. Once established, weeds compete with surrounding plants for the available light, water, and nutrients.

Weeds that have extensive root systems may be more efficient at getting nutrients from the soil than turfgrass plants. Plants with broad, flat leaves may also receive more fertilizer from liquid spray applications than narrow, vertically oriented grass blades, and may even shade out the turfgrass.

Methods for Managing Weeds

There are three primary methods of controlling weeds in home lawns. Each method, when used alone, will not usually control all of the weeds. The choice of weed control should match your desired level of lawn quality and your willingness to accept a lot of weeds or a few weeds in the lawn. If you wish to consistently control lawn weeds for an above-average or superior quality lawn, you must use a combination of all three methods.

Cultural Practices

Weeds tend to invade thin or bare areas, so the first line of defense is to follow cultural practices that favor the growth and development of a dense, healthy lawn. In addition to growing an adapted turfgrass, pay close attention to proper mowing, fertilizing, watering, and pest control.

As described in the "Selection" section on p. 1, grow an adapted grass in the right location in your landscape. Bermudagrass or bahiagrass will be weak and thin in shaded areas. Zoysiagrass or St. Augustinegrass would be better choices.

Mow at the recommended height for the turf-grass and at the right frequency. Mowing at the proper height will allow the grass to shade the soil and deprive weed seedlings from sunlight. Also, it encourages the root system to fully develop, which helps the grass tolerate summertime heat and stress. When cut too low, the lawn grass becomes weakened and less competitive, allowing weeds to become established. Remove no more than one-third of the grass height at any one mowing. Cutting off more than one-third at one time can stop the roots from growing, which is an open invitation to weeds.

Always mow with a sharp mower blade. Sharp blades cut the grass cleanly, which ensure rapid healing and regrowth. When dull blades tear and bruise the leaves, he wounded grass plants become weakened and less able to ward off marauding weeds.

Fertilize lawn grasses with the right amount of fertilizer based on soil test results and at the proper time of year. Avoid under- or overwatering, which can weaken the lawn and make it susceptible to invasions.

Insects and diseases may from time to time infest the lawn and damage the turfgrass. Damage from chinch bugs or a leaf spot disease, for instance, will cause the lawn to thin-out and become susceptible to weed invasion. These pests need to be controlled early to minimize the extent of damage.

Mechanical Methods

Many weed species do not tolerate frequent mowing. Several weeds can be controlled through non-chemical means. Some winter annuals, such as henbit and common chickweed, can be controlled by mowing. These weeds mature during the winter and bloom in the spring and die. Simply removing the flower by hand or by mowing will reduce the number of offspring in the fall. Perennial weeds such as dandelions and wild onions can be reduced through hand-weeding. Be sure to remove as much of the root stock as possible so the plant will not rejuvenate from these parts.

Following the one-third mowing rule and mowing at the recommended height will help limit the development of many weed species. Handpulling annual weeds is safe and effective. However, it is time-consuming and is not effective for the control of most perennial weeds. If you choose to handpull perennial weeds, such as dandelion, remove as much

of the root system as possible because the remaining pieces of rhizomes or roots will develop into new plants. Handpulling a "strange" or "new" weed when it first appears in the lawn will help to prevent the spread of that weed. Seed, sod, or plug areas left bare from weed removal to prevent future invasions.

Chemical Control--Herbicides

Use herbicides only when necessary and always in conjunction with a good turfgrass management program. Herbicides are applied at specific times of the year and will control only certain weed species. Also, many herbicides cannot be used on every turfgrass species. The herbicide label is the best reference for the safe and effective use of any herbicide. Always read the label before using any herbicide.

Before purchasing a herbicide, identify the problem weeds in your lawn. Grassy weeds, such as crabgrass, goosegrass, and annual bluegrass require different herbicides than broadleaf weeds, such as dandelion, shepherd's purse, and henbit. Applying a herbicide to control a weed it is not labelled for will be a waste of time and money.

Frequently, two or more herbicides are available that can control the same problem weed. Some factors to consider when comparing herbicides include the type of lawn grass, the risk of injury to the lawn or nearby shrubs and trees, the type of application equipment needed, environmental areas that may be affected, and the cost of treatment.

Turfgrass species vary in their tolerance to herbicides. Before applying any herbicide, check the label carefully for restrictions about the use of a herbicide on specific turfgrasses.

Another important consideration is the timing of a herbicide application in relation to the stage of growth of the weed and the lawn. Herbicides are formulated to work on certain growth stages of weeds. Apply **preemergence** herbicides to an existing turfgrass area before or at the same time weed seeds germinate to kill emerging weed seedlings. Apply **postemergence** herbicides to growing weeds after they have emerged from the soil.

Preemergence herbicides. Preemergence herbicides form a chemical barrier. As the weed seeds germinate, the developing shoots and roots contact and absorb the herbicide, resulting in death of the seedlings, usually by inhibition of root growth. So, it's important to uniformly apply the herbicide.

Preemergence herbicides should be applied according to the following schedule:

• **Fall**—When daytime temperatures drop to 55 to 60 °F at night, apply preemergence herbicides to control winter annual weeds, such as annual bluegrass, henbit, and common chickweed. Annual bluegrass germinates in late summer into early fall when air temperatures drop consistently into the mid-70s. This usually corresponds with September 15 to October 1 in coastal and central areas and September 1 to 15 in Piedmont and Mountain areas. Germination is earliest in weak turf areas such as shade or wet conditions. Additional annual bluegrass germination also occurs in early winter with warm days and cold nights.

• **Spring**—When daytime temperatures reach 65 to 70 °F for 4 to 5 days, apply preemergence herbicides to control summer annual weeds, such as crabgrass and goosegrass.

Crabgrass is a troublesome summer annual weed that germinates in the spring, matures and reproduces by seed in the summer, and then dies at the first killing frost in the fall. Crabgrass seed requires sunlight and moisture to germinate, so expect to find it in thin or weak stands of grass or in low, damp areas. Crabgrass is rarely found beneath the shaded canopies of trees or on the north side of buildings.

Crabgrass seed germination often coincides with the flowering of early spring plants such as redbuds, pears, crabapples, and forsythia. Approximate timing of application for preemergence crabgrass control are the first week of March in the Coastal Plain and Sandhill areas, and mid- to late March in the Piedmont and Mountains. Goosegrass germinates about 3 to 4 weeks later than crabgrass. Apply the preemergent herbicide uniformly across the lawn to establish a chemical barrier about a week before the crabgrass seeds are expected to germinate. Follow label directions, since many preemergent herbicides require at least $1/2$ inch of water after application to ensure that the chemical moves into the thatch and soil layer.

Some preemergent herbicides will break down during the summer months, so a repeat application may be necessary 2 months after the initial application to control any late-germinating crabgrass seeds.

Several preemergence herbicides are formulated with dry fertilizers to create fertilizer-herbicide mixtures called "weed 'n feed" products. Despite the convenience of controlling weeds and fertilizing the lawn, you should consider the kind of turfgrass growing in your lawn and the time of year before taking this approach. It may not be the appropriate time of year for a fertilizer application. For example, centipedegrass should not be fertilized in the spring until it fully greens up; however, waiting until the centipede has fully recovered from winter dormancy is too late to apply a preemergence herbicide since the weeds may already have emerged.

Labels provide specific restrictions and recommendations when using preemergence herbicides. Follow these general guidelines:
• Read the label for the specific time that must elapse before it is safe to seed.
• Do not use a preemergence herbicide at the time of turfgrass seeding, unless that is a labeled procedure. Severe injury can result if a preemergence herbicide is applied after seeding (examples: common bermudagrass, centipedegrass, fescues, and ryegrasses) or after sprigging (bermudagrass hybrids, centipedegrass, St. Augustinegrass, and zoysiagrasses).
• Mow new turfgrass seedlings at least three times before applying a preemergence herbicide.
• Do not apply a preemergence herbicide to the soil before laying sod.
• Return grass clippings to the lawn for two to three weeks after an application to help ensure that any herbicide adsorbed to the leaf blades is returned to the soil. Ideally, always return or recycle your clippings.

Postemergence herbicides. In contrast to preemergence herbicides, this group of herbicides controls only weeds that are emerged (seen) and actively growing at the time of treatment. Postemergence herbicides that are used to control weeds in lawns are absorbed and translocated or moved inside the plant. Therefore, you do not have to "drown" the weeds with a postemer-gence herbicide. Apply a postemergence herbicides only to the point of spray runoff. Any spray that runs off the weed is usually wasted and does not result in increased control.

Some herbicides, such as atrazine, have both preemergence and postemergence activity on a variety of annual broadleaf weeds. When these atrazine-fertilizer products are applied to centipede-grass or St. Augustinegrass *after* complete greenup, many annual broadleaf weeds can be controlled before or after they have already emerged.

Before applying any postemergence herbicide, read and understand the label.

To improve the weed control effectiveness of postemergence herbicides to control emerged annual weeds or when new growth or regrowth occurs on perennial weeds, and to improve the tolerance of turfgrass follow these guidelines:

1. **Apply postemergence herbicides in the fall and late spring.** The cooler temperatures will improve the turfgrass tolerance to herbicides. Also, perennial weeds and many annual weeds will be actively growing at this time of year, making them more easier to control. When using a postemergence herbicides, consider spot-treating problem areas instead of making a blanket application over the entire lawn.

2. **Do not apply postemergence herbicides to turfgrasses that are under stress from high temperatures or drought.** Turfgrasses become less tolerant to postemergent herbicides when air temperatures exceed 85 to 90 °F or when they are drought-stressed. Also, postemergent herbicides are less effective when applied to weeds that are stressed instead of actively growing.

3. **Do not apply a postemergent herbicide when the warm-season lawn is greening up in the spring.** Turfgrass grass that is coming out of winter dormancy is at greater risk of being injured from a postemergence herbicide than when it is fully dormant or actively growing.

Postemergence herbicides offer the best chemical control measure for broadleaf weeds. Most of the postemergence herbicides used to control broadleaf weeds are systemic (translocated) and foliar. They must remain on the weed leaves long enough to allow an adequate amount of chemical to penetrate leaves. If it rains before enough time has elapsed, weeds may not be affected by the application. Postemergent herbicides are most effective when weeds are young and actively growing and will readily translocate the chemical within the plant. Adequate soil moisture, high humidity, bright sunshine and air temperatures between 65 and 85 °F favor weed control. Control of biennial and perennial weeds is generally most effective when applying herbicides in spring to early summer or fall. Broadleaf weeds can also be controlled during the summer months; however, some turfgrasses are very sensitive to broadleaf herbicides, especially when under stress from heat and drought.

Summer annual broadleaf weeds, such as prostrate spurge, knotweed, and purslane, can be very difficult to control because they germinate over several weeks or months. Also, these weeds develop a thick waxy leaf as they mature that makes it difficult for the herbicide to enter the plant. For these hard-

When developing a weed management program, consider these approaches:

- Determine what types of turfgrass are present.
- Identify the problem weeds and note what time of year they appear. Past records of weed problems and weedy areas will help you to stay one step ahead of problem weeds.
- Determine the level of lawn quality you desire. Can you live with a few weeds? Do you have so many weeds that eliminating them will leave you with bare soil? If so, be prepared to establish a new lawn after you control the weeds.
- Weeds are usually the result of a poorly chosen or mismanaged turf. Plant the right turf species for your site. Determine why the weeds invaded the lawn. Some weeds are very specific in their site requirements and can provide clues about a particular site. For example, ground ivy, violets, chickweeds and moss are very shade-tolerant; knotweed and goosegrass grows in compacted soils; prostrate spurge grows in hot locations with high soil temperatures (that is, along sidewalks and driveways). See Table 15 for a list of site conditions and the kinds of weeds that are found.
- Follow a good turf management program. The most effective, long-term solution to minimizing weed problems is a healthy, dense lawn obtained through proper turf management. If herbicides are not accompanied by basic improvements in the turf management program, weeds will probably reinfest the area, or be replaced by other weeds that are more difficult to control.
- If a herbicide is needed, select a chemical that is effective for the weeds and safe for the turfgrass. Follow all label directions and apply the herbicide at the proper rate and time. Survey the site for sensitive areas, and consider the factors of drift and off-site movement of pesticides.
- Monitor the effectiveness of the weed control program. If you had poor results from a herbicide application, try to determine why the failure occurred. Always be on the lookout for herbicide damage to desirable plants. In some instances, damage may warrant a change in application rate or another herbicide.

to-control weeds, consider a nonchemical approach. Mow at the recommended height, water properly, provide adequate fertility, and reestablish thin lawn areas by reseeding or sodding.

Application Equipment. Applying herbicides successfully requires that you use the right equipment and application technique. The amount of herbicide that needs to be applied to the lawn will be listed on the label. For home lawns, the recommended rate will often be given in an amount (pounds, fluid or dry ounces) of product per 1,000 sq. ft. of lawn area.

Apply the recommended rate. Avoid following the adage that "if a little is good, then a lot more is better," since herbicides can severely injure the lawn grasses when excessive amounts are applied.

Use the right equipment to apply the herbicide evenly and uniformly to the lawn. If you apply too much spray or overlap too much with granular products, the increase in herbicide can also lead to an increased risk of turfgrass injury. On the other hand, if the spray or granule application does not overlap, there are areas of the lawn that won't be treated which often results in streaks of weeds in the lawn.

Liquid formulations of herbicides are diluted with water and then sprayed on the lawn. Commonly used equipment for liquid products are hand-held pump-up sprayers and hose-end applicators. You need to know the square footage of your lawn to apply the herbicide at the correct rate. Before application, measure your lawn to determine its square footage so you can then determine how much herbicide would be required to cover that area.

Granular herbicides can be applied with a drop-type or rotary spreader. To ensure uniform distribution and to help prevent any skips or excessive overlap, divide the required amount in half. Apply one-half the required amount in one direction and the remaining amount at right angles to the first.

Herbicide safety precautions. Always read and follow label directions regarding the handling and application of the herbicide. Mix and use only the amount of herbicide that you need to treat the lawn. Store the herbicide in its original container. Place them in dry areas protected from freezing temperatures. Finally, keep herbicides out of the reach of children, pets, and livestock.

For more information about the use, handling, storage, and disposal of pesticides, visit Clemson University's Pesticide Information Program at http://entweb.clemson.edu/pesticid/saftyed/homeuse.htm.

Read labels carefully for instructions when using postemergence herbicides. Also, follow these guidelines:

- Avoid applications when rain is expected. If rainfall occurs soon after application, the application may not be effective.
- Delay mowing a treated area for at least three days after application.
- Delay applications to newly seeded areas until grass is mowed at least three times.
- Delay seeding bare spots left by weeds until three weeks have passed and the area has received rain or irrigation to break down any herbicide remaining in the soil.
- Delay applying a herbicide to a newly sodded area for four to six weeks. Check the label.
- Carefully operate application equipment and monitor weather conditions to prevent spray drift and herbicide vapor during application.
- Apply postemergence herbicides in the fall and late spring months. Air temperatures are cooler at this time of year, resulting in better turfgrass tolerance to herbicides. Also, perennial weeds and many annual weeds are actively growing during these times of the year and are easier to control with postemergence herbicides.
- Do not apply postemergence herbicides to turfgrasses and weeds that are stressed due to high air temperatures or drought. Turfgrass tolerance to postemergence herbicides decreases at air temperatures greater than 90 °F or when turfgrasses are drought-stressed. Also, weed control is poorer when herbicides are applied to weeds in a stressed condition than when applied to actively growing weeds.
- Do not apply postemergence herbicides during spring greenup (the time when winter-dormant grasses are resuming active growth) of warm-season turfgrasses. The risk of injury from postemergence herbicides is greater during the greenup process than when the turfgrass is fully dormant or actively growing.

Insect Management*

Several insects and related pests are common in lawns (Table 16). **Southern chinch bugs, spittlebugs, grass scales** and **bermudagrass mites** suck plant juices. **Mole crickets, white grubs** and **billbugs** live in the soil and damage the grass roots. Other pests, including **sod webworms, grass loopers, cutworms** and **armyworms**, eat the grass leaves. Additional insects and related pests such as fleas, millipedes, chiggers, sowbugs and snails do not damage the lawn, but may become nuisances by biting people or crawling into houses, garages and swimming pools.

Cultural Practices

Over the past several years, studies have demonstrated that the need for pesticide applications to control lawn pests, such as chinch bugs, sod webworms, and armyworms, can be drastically reduced by following certain cultural practices. A properly managed lawn can tolerate more damage before symptoms are evident.

Following proper lawn management practices may reduce the number of pests that cause damage to the turf or allow the grass to tolerate more damage before symptoms are evident.

Fertilize the lawn at the recommended rate for the specific species you are growing. Excessive nitrogen fertilizer, particularly those high in quickly available, water soluble nitrogen, will increase the succulence of the turf. This will make the turfgrass more attractive to some insects. When possible, use fertilizers that contain a slow release nitrogen source.

Proper mowing practices will also aid in pest reduction. Mow the grass at the proper height and frequency using a sharp mower blade.

Improper mowing, excessive watering and fertilizing can cause lawngrasses to develop a thick, spongy mat of live, dead and dying shoots, stems and roots which accumulate in a layer above the soil surface. This spongy mat, referred to as thatch, is an excellent habitat for chinch bugs and turf caterpillars, and chemically ties up insecticides, therefore reducing their effectiveness. When a serious thatch problem exists, it may be necessary to remove the thatch mechanically by vertical mowing or power raking. Avoid excessive thatch and mechanically dethatch your lawn when it is needed. Thatch is generally caused by overwatering and overfertilizing.

Monitor your lawn frequently for signs of insect damage. If you suspect a damaging insect is present, make a proper diagnosis and, if needed, apply a recommended chemical treatment at the proper rate. Early detection and control will lessen the chance of losing a large quantity of turfgrass.

Biological Control

Several predatory and parasitic insects are often associated with chinch bugs and webworms. The most prominent predator of chinch bugs is the big-eyed bug (Figure 21). One of the earwigs (*Labidura*) is a very good predator of both chinch bugs and webworm larvae as well as several other turfgrass insects.

Spiders and ground beetles are efficient predators of several harmful lawn insects and are considered extremely beneficial. An ichneumonid wasp is also a common parasite of the webworm larvae and can be seen hovering over infested areas.

The fungus *Beauveria* causes a disease in which fungal threads fill the body cavity of chinch bugs, causing death in about three days. The beneficial nematode, *Steinernema carpocapsae*, also attacks mole crickets. Other beneficial nematodes help control sod webworms, billbugs, cutworms and armyworms. The presence of these beneficial organisms will often prevent insect pests from reaching damaging levels.

Chemical Control

Insecticides labelled for home lawns are available in several formulations: baits, emulsifiable concentrates, wettable powders, soluble powders, and granules. The formulation selected, as well as the specific insecticide chosen, determine the level of control. For example, bait formulations are superior in late summer and fall for mole cricket control, whereas spring and summer treatments with sprays or granules give better control. For specific insecticide recommendations on lawns, consult the Home and Garden Information Center (1-888-656-9988).

Apply insecticides properly. Read and understand all directions on the container label regarding dosage rates, application information, and precautions. When a spray is applied for controlling insects, it is important to apply the insecticide in a large amount of water. The jar attachment to a garden hose is the suggested application device for

---

*Adapted from Clyde Gorsuch, Ph.D., "Insect Control," *Southern Lawns*.

Table 16

Periods of insect activity and treatment timing chart for South Carolina[1].

Expected Time of Insect Occurrence

	Jan	Feb	Mar	Apr	May	June	July	Aug	Sept	Oct	Nov	Dec
Fire ants			████████████████████████████████									
Fall armyworm						███████████████████ Present ████████ Control █████					
Bees and wasps			████████████████████████████████████									
Chinch bugs					Nymphs and adults							
Cutworms			████████████████████████████████████									
White grubs (Green June beetle, Japanese, Asiatic)			Larvae			Adults		Larvae				
Mole crickets			Nymphs and adults / Baits[2]									
Sod webworms					Larvae							
Spittlebugs and leafhoppers												

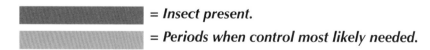

 ████████████████ = *Insect present.*

 ████████████████ = *Periods when control most likely needed.*

[1]*Periods of activity will vary up to 3 weeks from the Mountains to the Coast.*
[2]*Baits are effective at this time.*

lawns. Choose the type that requires 15 to 20 gallons of water passing through the hose to empty the quart size jars. Put the amount of insecticide in the jar as directed on the label for 1,000 ft. Fill the jar the rest of the way with water. Spray the contents over 1,000 sq. ft. of lawn area. To insure even coverage, spray back and forth across the measured area; then turn at right angles and spray back and forth across the same area.

To help prevent unnecessary environmental contamination and reduction of beneficial insects, make spot-treatments when you first notice infestations and the damaged area is small. Treat the off-color area and about a ten-foot buffer area surrounding it.

If damage is widespread over the yard or if many infested areas are detected, treat the entire lawn. Inspect the area two to three times at biweekly intervals to determine if the infestation is under control.

Precautions When Using Pesticides

Read the manufacturer's label carefully before opening the pesticide container and follow all instructions and precautions. Store pesticides locked up in original labeled containers, and out of reach of children. Triple rinse empty containers and put rinse water in spray tank. To dispose of the empty container (1 gallon or smaller), wrap in newspaper, crush or puncture to prevent reuse, and put in garbage can for disposal in an approved sanitary landfill.

Detecting and Identifying Turfgrass Insects

Look for pests before serious infestations ravage your lawn. Look for damaged, injured areas, sod torn up by animals feeding on insects, the presence of moths flying over the lawn at night, and birds frequenting a particular area of the lawn are all conditions that provide clues concerning lawn pests. By detecting and identifying insect pests early, you have sufficient time to correctly identify the pest, choose an appropriate control, and apply controls before severe damage occurs.

Insects are only a few of the many causes of yellowish or brownish areas in grass. Disease, nematodes, dry weather and nutritional disorders can sometimes cause this injury. Be sure of the cause so the proper treatment can be applied to correct the trouble without the needless use of pesticides and extensive damage to the grass.

Figure 21

(Left) big-eyed bug and (right) earwig (Labidura).

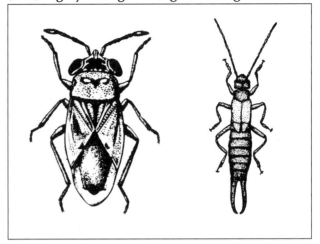

If you suspect an insect pest, use a sampling technique that will capture the insect causing the damage. The sampling technique must be matched to the type of insect that may be present as described in the "Turfgrass Insect Pests" section.

A few common turfgrass insect pests in South Carolina are described in the next few pages. Additional information on turfgrass insects can be found at the Clemson Entomology Insect Information (http://entweb.clemson.edu/cuentres/index.htm) and the HGIC (http://hgic.clemson.edu) web sites.

Insect Pests Found on Leaves and Stems

Sod Webworms and Fall Armyworms

Various caterpillars, primarily the sod webworm and fall armyworm, are pests of lawn grasses in South Carolina. Sod webworm adults are small, dingy-brown moths with a wingspread of about $^3/_4$ in. (Figure 22). Sod webworm adult moths have a characteristic snout-like projection in front of their heads. They fly over the grass in the evening. Larvae are small, greenish caterpillars with many black spots and range from $^1/_{25}$ in long when they first emerge from the egg to about $^3/_4$ in. long when mature.

Fall armyworm adults are light brown moths with a wingspread of about $1^1/_2$ in. Mature caterpillars are about $1^1/_2$ in. long when mature. Upon hatching, fall armyworm larvae are more grayish-green than webworms and have a stripe along their sides (Figure 23). When approaching maturity, they are pale brown to black with large stripes along their sides. On the front of the head is a yellow inverted "Y" marking. Its life cycle is about the same as that of the sod webworm.

Sod webworm and fall armyworm larvae, as with other lawn caterpillars, feed on all species of warm-season turfgrasses including bermuda, St. Augustine, centipede, zoysia, and bahiagrass. The newly hatched webworm larvae chew away tissue from the surface of the grass blades, leaving a colorless, membranous area on the leaves. As larvae mature, the grass is progressively chewed off and becomes ragged and yellowish to brownish in color. Damaged areas are often first noticed along hedges and flower beds. Injury normally begins in a few spots with the injured areas being only 2 or 3 in. across. When heavy infestations are present, these spots enlarge, coalesce, and may encompass large areas of the lawn. Severely damaged grass under stress due to hot, dry weather may be killed. However, if infested grass is not allowed to suffer from lack of moisture, it can recover from a large amount of webworm feeding.

Armyworm injury is similar to that of webworms; however, the damage is usually more scattered and not confined to patches as with sod webworm infestations. It is not unusual to have populations of armyworms, webworms, and other lawn caterpillars all feeding at the same time in the same location.

Studies during the past several years have demonstrated that following certain management practices can drastically reduce the need for pesticide applications to control lawn caterpillars.

Cultural Practices

Cultural practices can influence the susceptibility of lawn grasses to webworms and armyworms. Rapid growth, resulting from applications of fast-release, water-soluble, inorganic nitrogen fertilizers,

Figure 22

Sod webworm larva and adult.

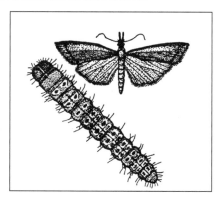

substantially increase chances of lawn caterpillar attacks. The lush succulent growth attracts egg-laying female moths. Damage from these pests can be greatly reduced with minimum applications of slow-release nitrogen fertilizers.

Excessive watering or fertilization can cause lawn grasses to develop a thick, spongy mat of live, dead, and dying shoots, stems, and roots which accumulate in a layer above the soil surface. This spongy mat, referred to as thatch, is an excellent habitat for lawn caterpillars, and also chemically ties up insecticides, thereby reducing their effectiveness. When a serious thatch problem exists, it may be necessary to remove the thatch mechanically by vertical mowing or power raking.

Proper mowing practices can make the grass more tolerant to lawn caterpillars and greatly improve the appearance of the lawn. Mow your lawn at the proper height with a sharp mower blade. Also, mow often enough so that no more than one-third of the leaf blade is removed at each mowing. Leave the clippings on the lawn.

Monitoring

Inspect the lawn every week during the spring, especially during the summer and fall months. Look for adults flying over the grass in the evening. To check the lawn for caterpillars, examine grass in off-color areas to determine if the blades have a chewed appearance. Part the grass in the suspected areas and closely examine the soil surface.

Sod webworm larvae rest in a curled position on the soil surface during the day and feed only at night or during cloudy or rainy periods. Small green pellets of excrement will be numerous on the soil surface when the insects are present. Armyworms do not rest in a curled position but feed during the day and may be seen crawling over the grass.

If no sod webworm or armyworm larvae are noticed by parting the grass, their presence or absence can be confirmed by applying a soap mixture. Mix 1 to 2 fl. oz. liquid dishwashing detergent per gallon of water and drench 2 sq. ft. with this solution. Observe the area for about 2 minutes. If any caterpillars are present, they will emerge to the grass surface and can be detected. If no caterpillars are found in the first area checked, examine at least three or four places in suspected areas. In most areas of South Carolina it is usually August before damage occurs. Some years, populations do not become damaging. In spite of its name, the fall armyworm is usually the first species to be troublesome in lawns.

Figure 23

Young, immature armyworm.

There are other factors such as disease, nutritional imbalances, and drought that will result in off-color areas in lawns. Examine the lawn carefully to determine if any corrective measures are needed.

Beneficial Insects

A number of beneficial insects and spiders are extremely efficient in reducing lawn caterpillar populations. A predaceous earwig, several spiders, ground beetles, and parasitic wasps are some of the more common predators and parasites found associated with lawn caterpillars. Quite often these are misidentified as pests, and are unnecessarily treated with pesticides. This elimination of beneficial organisms can lead to a caterpillar problem.

Control With Pesticides

When it is established that lawn caterpillars are the problem, and that the damage threshold of 10 to 12 larvae per sq. ft. has been reached, consider applying a pesticide. A microbial insecticide called *Bt* (*Bacillus thuringiensis*) is a biological control agent which only kills caterpillars.

Apply the insecticide properly. Read and understand all directions on the container label regarding dosage rates, application information, and precautions. When you use a spray it is important to apply the insecticide in a large amount of water. The jar attachment for a garden hose is the suggested lawn sprayer for homeowners. The type that requires 15 to 20 gallons of water passing through the hose to empty the quart-sized jar is recommended. Put the amount of insecticide in the jar as directed on the label for 1,000 sq. ft., fill the jar with water, and spray the contents over 1,000 sq. ft. of lawn. To insure even coverage, spray back and forth across the same area.

Granular formulations of the recommended insecticides may be substituted for sprays. Granules should be applied with a drop-type sprayer rather than the cyclone type to avoid getting granules on sidewalks and driveways. After application of granules, irrigate lightly with about $\frac{1}{8}$ inch of water.

To further avoid environmental contamination and reduction of beneficial insects, spot treatments can be applied when infestations are first noticed and the damaged area is very small. Treat the off-color area and about a five-foot buffer area surrounding it. When damage is widespread or many infested areas are detected, the entire lawn should be treated. Inspect the area two to three times at biweekly intervals to determine if the infestations are under control. Caution: Worms treated with *Bt* may require 2 to 5 days to die, but they are unable to feed after the first day.

Spittlebugs
Identification

Adult two-lined spittlebugs are black with red eyes and legs and have two orange transverse stripes across their wings (Figure 24). They are about $\frac{1}{4}$ in. long. The nymphs are yellow or white in color with a brown head. They are enveloped in a mass of white frothy spittle that they excrete for protection. Both adults and nymphs suck juices from the grass with their piercing-sucking mouthparts; however, research has shown that damage is caused primarily by the adults through the injection of phytotoxic salivary substances. Adults are most active during the early morning hours; during the heat of the day they retreat to the soil surface.

Spittlebugs attack all turfgrass species, but centipedegrass appears to be their favorite host. Adults also feed on landscape plants, especially hollies.

Eggs are laid at the base of the grass in the thatch, in hollow grass stems, or behind the leaf

Figure 24

Spittlebug adult.

Figure 25

Nymphs enveloped in a protective spittle mass.

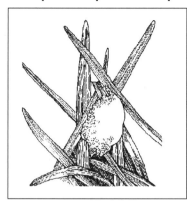

sheaths. There are five nymphal stages and the life cycle requires about 2 months. There are two generations per year. Eggs laid by the second generation overwinter and hatch the following spring. Depending upon temperature and precipitation, most of the overwintering eggs hatch from late March to late April. The first generation adults are abundant in June. The adult population peaks again in early August to early September.

The majority of the spittle masses (Figure 25) are not readily visible as they are usually located near the soil surface or in the thatch area. Infested turf wilts and the tips turn yellow and eventually brown then curl. Spittlebugs require high humidity conditions for optimum development. Thatch contributes to these conditions. Follow approved practices regarding mowing, fertilization, and irrigation to reduce thatch buildup. If a thatch problem exists, dethatching will reduce spittlebug problems.

Chinch Bugs
Identification

The southern chinch bug is the most injurious insect pest of St. Augustinegrass. It is not a serious pest on any of the other lawn grasses.
Adults are about $^1/_5$ inch long, light in color with small black triangular patches on the wings. The wings are carried folded over the back. The nymphs are from $^1/_{20}$ to $^1/_5$ inch long and vary in color from a reddish with a white band across the back to black as they near adult size.

Life cycle

Eggs begin hatching about the middle of April each year. Expect three to four generations of southern chinch bugs. The nymphs or immature chinch bugs are about the size of a pinhead when

they hatch and they molt five times before reaching the adult stage (Figure 26). The small nymphs are bright red with a white band across the back. Late stage nymphs and adult chinch bugs are about $^1/_5$ in. long and black; the adults have white wings.

Southern chinch bugs suck the plant juices from grass resulting in yellowish to brownish patches in the lawns. These injured areas are often first noticed in water stressed areas along edges of lawns.

The eggs are laid in leaf sheaths or crevices in leaf nodes and other protected places. Upon hatching, the nymphs, which cause most of the damage, suck sap from the grass and inject a toxin that causes the leaves to turn yellow and die. As the grass dies the chinch bugs move to healthy grass, leaving the killed grass in their wake. As they feed, they cause the dead areas to slowly enlarge. The nymphs develop into adults in 4 to 6 weeks. Expect three to four generations a year.

Chinchbug damage is usually greatest during hot, dry weather, especially July and August, and in sunny areas rather than in the shade. High levels of nitrogen and thick thatch layers predispose turfgrasses to chinch bug attacks

Detection

The most critical time for turf damage by chinch bugs is July and August. During this period the turf is frequently under moisture stress and the feeding activity of chinch bugs is greatest. The combined effects of these two stress factors is often more than a home lawn can withstand. Early stages of chinch bug nymphs are not easily seen, and damage symptoms are not severe enough to be noticeable. Close observation of susceptible turf during early June is critical

Figure 26

Chinch bug growth stages from immature (left) to adult (right). Note their extremely small size.

Credit: Don Short.

in detecting chinch bugs before damage occurs. St. Augustine lawns as well as bermudagrass and zoysiagrass should be closely observed for chinch bugs, especially if the pest has been observed during previous years. Since chinch bugs usually occur in scattered patches, particular attention should be given to areas where damage was observed in previous years.

Inspect the lawn every week during the spring, summer, and fall months. Look for off-color areas, especially in portions of the lawn that are not shaded by trees, and along sidewalks and driveways. Chinchbug damage can be easily confused with drought: chinch bugs cause the leaves to turn a yellowish-orange straw color while drought makes the leaves turn a grayish-brown straw color. Also, there are other factors that will cause off-color areas to appear in the lawn, such as diseases and nutritional deficiencies. Therefore, carefully examine the lawn to determine the cause of the problem and what corrective measures are needed.

Usually when chinch bugs are present in sufficient numbers to begin causing yellowish areas in lawns, they can be found by parting the grass at the margin of the yellowed areas and closely examining the soil surface and base of the turf. Examine several places in suspect areas. In heavy infestations, the bugs may be seen crawling over the grass blades and sidewalks.

If no chinch bugs are noticed by visual inspection of the grass, their presence or absence can be confirmed by flushing them out with water. Here's how:

1. Cut out both ends of a metal can, such as a 2- or 3-lb. coffee can. Push one end about 2 or 3 inches into the soil at the edge of the yellowish areas of grass. If it is difficult to pass the can through the St. Augustinegrass runners, a knife may be used to cut a circle in the grass the size of the can.

2. Fill the can with water. If bugs are present, the adults and nymphs will float to the top within 5 minutes. It may be necessary to add more water to keep the level above the grass surface.

If bugs are not found in the first area checked, examine at least 3 or 4 additional places in the suspected areas. Take action if you find 25 to 30 insects per square foot of lawn area.

Cultural Practices

Cultural practices can influence the susceptibility of St. Augustinegrass to chinch bugs. Rapid growth resulting from frequent applications of water soluble inorganic nitrogen fertilizers increase the chance of chinch bug attack. Chinch bug problems can be greatly reduced with minimum applications of slow-release nitrogen fertilizers.

Prolonged periods of moisture stress can encourage southern chinch bug problems. Watch the lawn closely and when the edges of the grass leaves start curling and appear to have a dull bluish-gray color, water the lawn immediately with ⅔ in of water. Do not irrigate again until wilting begins to occur.

Excessive water or fertilization can cause St. Augustinegrass lawns to develop a thick, spongy mat of live, dead and dying shoots, stems, and roots which accumulate in a layer above the soil surface. This spongy mat, referred to as thatch, is an excellent habitat for chinch bugs. The thatch provides a home for chinch bugs and chemically ties up insecticides and therefore reduces control. When a serious thatch problem exists, it may be necessary to remove the thatch mechanically by vertical mowing or power raking.

Proper mowing practices can make the grass more tolerant to chinch bugs and greatly improve the appearance of the lawn. St. Augustinegrass should be mowed to a height of 3 to 4 inches. It is very important to keep the mower blade sharpened. The grass should be mowed often enough so that no more than one-third of the height is reduced at each mowing. Recycle the clippings back into the lawn.

Resistant St. Augustinegrass Varieties

St. Augustine varieties Floratam, Floralawn and Floratine provide varying degrees of resistance to chinch bug feeding. Most chinch bugs cannot complete their development when attempting to feed on 'Floratam' or 'Floralawn'. If a new lawn is being established or an old one replaced, consider the use of 'Floratam' or 'Floralawn'. In comparison studies with other established varieties ('Bitterblue', 'Roselawn', 'Scott's 1081', 'Seville', 'Raleigh' and 'Florida Common'), 'Floratam' and 'Floralawn' showed resistance to the southern chinch bug. 'Floratam' and 'Floralawn' exhibit true antibiosis and are resistant to chinch bug injury, while 'Floratine' is only tolerant to low populations.

Beneficial Insects

Several predatory insects are often associated with southern chinch bugs. The most prominent predator of chinch bugs is the black big-eyed bug. A predacious earwig is also a very good predator on all stages of the chinch bug. An adult earwig has been observed to eat as many as 50 adult chinch bugs in one night. Big-eyed bugs and anthocorids (another group of predators) are about the same size as chinch bugs and are often confused with them. Quite often these beneficial insects are misidenti-fied as chinch bugs, and a pesticide is applied when it is not needed.

Control With Pesticides

When it is established that chinch bugs are the problem and the damage threshold of 25 to 30 chinch bugs per square foot has been reached, a pesticide is warranted. Apply the insecticide properly. Read and understand all directions on the container label regarding dosage rates, application information, and precautions. When a spray is used, apply the insecticide in a large amount of water. The jar attachment to a garden hose is the suggested application device for homeowners. Use the type that requires 15 to 20 gals. of water passing through the hose to empty the quart-sized jar. Put the amount of insecticide in the jar as directed on the label for 1,000 sq. ft. Fill the jar the rest of the way with water. Spray-out the contents over 1,000 sq. ft. of lawn. To insure even coverage, spray back and forth across the same area. The treated grass should be irrigated lightly to flush the insecticide into the thatch layer where the chinch bugs are feeding.

Granular formulations of the recommended insecticides may be substituted for sprays. Granules should be applied with a drop-type spreader rather than the cyclone type to avoid getting granules on sidewalks and driveways. Irrigate lightly with about $1/_8$ in. of water. A correctly applied application should provide control of chinch bugs for 8 to 10 weeks.

To further avoid environmental contamination and reduction of beneficial insects, spot treatments can be applied when infestations are first noticed and the damaged area is very small. Treat the off-color area and about a 5-foot buffer area surrounding it. Inspect the area 2 to 3 times at biweekly intervals to determine if the infestation is under control. If damage is widespread over the yard or if many infested areas are detected, the entire yard should be treated.

To preserve beneficial arthropods, spot treat the damaged area and 5 to 10 ft. beyond. Recheck in 2 to 3 days. Spot treat again, if needed.

Insects in Thatch and Soil

Ground Pearls
Identification

Ground pearls are scale insects that live in the soil and suck the juices from the grass roots (Figure 27). Centipedegrass is most commonly attacked, but infestations have been found in bahiagrass, St. Augustinegrass and carpetgrass.

Life cycle. The eggs are laid in the soil during April and May. The eggs hatch into tiny crawlers which move about until they locate a feeding site. Then they insert their tiny beaks into the grass roots and begin secreting a hard, yellow-brown scaly covering which completely encloses their bodies. They are round in shape and range in size from a grain of sound to about $1/_6$ inch in diameter (Figure 28). They look very much like small pearls, hence their name.

The adult egg-laying female which emerges from the "pearl" is about $1/_6$ inch long, pink in color and has well developed forelegs and claws to enable her to move through the soil. Adult males are rarely seen, but resemble a tiny gnat. The life cycle from egg to adult takes at least one year and possibly up to two years.

Detection

Symptoms attributed to ground pearl injury are first a yellowing of the grass, followed by browning.

Figure 27

Ground pearls on centipedegrass roots.

Figure 28

Closeup of ground pearls compared to the size of a match head.

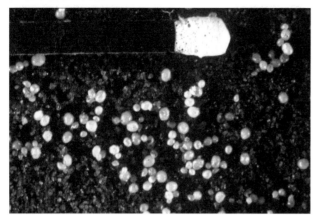

Ground pearl damage becomes most noticeable when the grass is under stress due to drought, nutritional deficiencies, etc. Under stressful conditions, the grass may not be able to withstand the damaging effects of the pearls and the grass will die. On the other hand, properly watered and otherwise well-managed lawns often do not show noticeable damage, even though they are heavily infested with these insects. There are other factors such as disease, nutritional imbalances, drought, and nematodes (especially in centipedegrass) that will cause off-color areas in lawns. The lawn should be carefully examined to determine what is causing the damage before treating the lawn to correct the problem.

Control

All approved practices regarding fertilization, watering and mowing should be carried out to keep the grass growing ahead of the damage. At the present time it is felt that the benefits gained from an insecticide treatment for ground pearls is not sufficient to warrant an application. This is based on past research and grass response to insecticide treatments.

Mole Crickets
Identification

Mole crickets are serious lawn pests in the sandy soils of the Coastal Plain. The southern and tawny mole crickets are two of the most destructive species (Figure 29). The tawny mole cricket is dark brown and can reach $1\frac{1}{2}$ inches in length; southern mole crickets are smaller and grayer. Both species possess the formidable digging claws on their front legs that earn their name.

Mole crickets damage lawns by tunneling through the soil and uprooting plants, causing them to dry out and die. The tawny mole cricket actually feeds on grass, while the southern mole cricket is primarily a carnivore, feeding on insects and earthworms.

Most of the damage occurs in late summer and fall as nymphs reach maturity. However, the overwintering adults will be tunneling in late winter and spring. The damage subsides in the spring when eggs are laid and the adults die. It's usually midsummer before further damage is noted.

Life Cycle

Mole crickets deposit their eggs in chambers hollowed out in the soil. Most chambers are found in the upper 6 in. of soil, but cool temperatures and/or dry soil cause the chambers to be constructed at a greater depth. An average female will excavate three to five egg chambers and deposit about 35 eggs per cell.

In most locations, egg-laying by tawny and southern mole crickets usually begins in the latter part of March, with peak egg-laying in May through mid-June (Figure 30). About three-quarters of the eggs are laid during these months. Peak egg hatch normally occurs during the first half of June in most locations. Egg hatch occurs from mid-June through July. The young nymphs escape from the egg chamber and burrow to the soil surface to begin feeding on organic material and on other small organisms including insects.

Most mole cricket feeding occurs at night during warm weather, after rain showers or irrigation. All nymphal stages as well as adults come to the surface at night to search for food. Tunneling of more than 20 inches per night has been observed. During the

Figure 29

Southern (left) and tawny mole cricket (right).

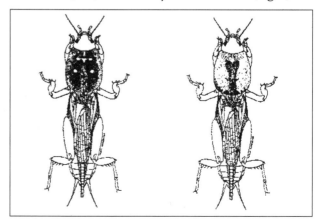

Figure 30

Typical mole cricket activity periods in South Carolina.

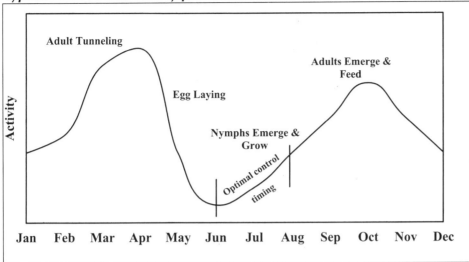

In late June and early July, sample your lawn for mole cricket nymphs. They will be small and their tunneling activity will not be readily evident. Early in the morning or late in the afternoon, use a soap flush to sample the damaged areas that you previously observed in the spring. Mix 1 to 2 fl. oz. of liquid dishwashing detergent per gal. of water and apply with a sprinkling can to 2 sq. ft. of lawn in several areas (Figure 31). The detergent solution irritates the mole crickets which forces them to the surface. Newly hatched mole crickets are only about $^3/_4$ inch long and tend to disappear quickly once coming to the surface. If an average of two to four mole cricket nymphs appear on the surface within 3 minutes, then an insecticide treatment is probably needed.

day the mole crickets return to their permanent burrows and may remain there for long periods of time when unfavorable weather conditions prevail. Adult mole crickets are strongly attracted to lights during their spring dispersal flights.

Detection

In late winter and early spring look for the burrowing and tunneling activity of the adult mole crickets. Map or mark these areas for potential treatment with an insecticide, because these are the locations where most of their offspring will be found in midsummer. Although you can control the adults with an insecticide, it is best to wait until the summer to control the young nymphs which are most sensitive to insecticide applications.

Cultural Control

Proper mowing, irrigation, and fertility practices can encourage a deep, healthy root system which is more tolerant to soil-inhabiting insects. Do not mow shorter than the recommended heights listed in Table 10 on p. 31. Keep the mower blade sharp.

Do not allow turf to dry out excessively. When irrigation is required, apply $^3/_4$ in. water. Do not irrigate again until the grass begins to wilt to encourage deep root growth.

Fertilize according to soil test results. Maintain an appropriate soil pH and adequate levels of potassium and minor nutrients.

Natural and Biological Controls

Southern mole crickets are very cannibalistic. Young nymphs will devour each other and the unhatched eggs.

When mole crickets come to the soil surface they are subject to numerous predators, including fire ants, ground beetles, *Labidura* earwigs, and *Lycosa* spiders. Larger animals including raccoons, skunks, red foxes, and armadillos also feed on mole crickets, but often damage lawns when searching for them.

Figure 31

Soap-flush technique to determine the presence of certain insects in turf, such as chinch bugs and mole crickets.

Concentrated biological control research is under way concerning the introduction of several mole cricket parasites from South America. A parasitic nematode (*Steinernema scapterisci*) patented by the University of Florida will be commercially available. It only attacks foreign mole crickets. The nematodes live in the soil and enter the mole cricket through openings in the body. Once inside, they release bacteria that feed on the mole cricket, usually killing it within 48 hours. The nematodes feed on the bacteria and reproduce inside the mole cricket.

A parasitic fly is being evaluated and is now established in certain areas. Laboratory and quarantine work is continuing with other natural enemies including fungal pathogens, a predatory larva of a beetle, and a pathogenic virus, all from South America.

Chemical Control

If damage occurred the previous year or if excessive tunneling (egg-laying activity) was noticed in the spring months, a pesticide application will probably be required. The major effort should be directed toward young nymphs. These treatments should be applied in June, July, and early August when the nymphs are most sensitive to treatments. Mid- to late June is the optimum time for an application in most locations.

Before applying a pesticide, inspect the lawn for tunneling activity. If none is noticed, confirm the presence or absence of mole crickets by using the soap flush technique described earlier. If a pesticide is warranted, the best time for controlling the small nymphs is in late June and July.

Mole crickets can be controlled by sprays, granules, or baits. Treat the lawn when the overnight temperature is expected to be 60 °F or above. The lawn should be moist prior to treatment. If it has become dry, irrigate the area to be treated by running sprinklers for about an hour. This helps the sprays or granules penetrate into the soil. In the case of baits, moisture encourages the mole crickets to come to the surface to feed on the bait.

Apply all pesticides as late in the day as possible. Where a range of rates are given, use the high rate for adult mole cricket control.

Be sure the pesticide is labeled for lawns. Read and understand all directions on the container label regarding dosage rates, application information, and precautions. When a spray is used, apply the insecticide in a large amount of water. The jar attachment to a garden hose is the suggested application device for homeowners. The type that requires 15 to 20 gals. of water passing through the hose to empty the quart-sized jar is recommended. Put the amount of insecticide in the jar as directed on the label for 1,000 sq. ft. Fill the remainder of jar the rest of the way with water. Spray the contents over 1,000 sq. ft. of lawn. To insure even coverage, spray back and forth across the same area.

Some granular or liquid insecticides must be irrigated immediately after application with $\frac{1}{2}$ inch of water to leach the insecticide into the top 1 to 2 inches of soil. Refer to the label instructions.

If a bait is used, apply it preferably in late afternoon or in early evening and when it is unlikely to rain overnight. Scatter the bait thinly and evenly over the soil surface. To insure even coverage, spread the bait back and forth across a measured area, then turn at right angles and spread back and forth across the same area again. A few flakes should fall on every square inch of soil in the infested areas. If distributing the bait by hand, be sure to wear rubber gloves. Do not irrigate after application.

White Grubs and Billbugs
Identification

White grubs are the larval stages of a certain family of beetles called scarab beetles. They include Japanese beetles, green June beetles, Asiatic garden beetles, and northern and southern masked chafers (Figure 32). The adult beetles feed on the leaves of trees and other plants. These plump grubs have a distinctive brown head and usually lie in a curled

Figure 32

Various white grub larvae and adults that are found in lawns.

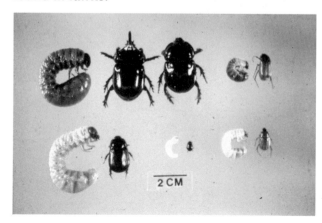

Figure 33

Characteristic "C"-shaped white grub larva.

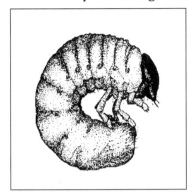

or C-shaped position. (Figure 33). They are dirty-white in color with brown heads and with dark areas visible at the rear of the abdomen. Most have rather long life cycles with the grub stages lasting from several months to two or three years.

Adult billbugs are snout beetles. The beetles are black and about $^3/_8$ in. long when mature. The white, legless larvae have hard, yellowish- or reddish-brown heads (Figure 34). Billbugs are found most often on zoysiagrass, but also may attack bermudagrass and other grasses. The larval stage does the most damage, but both adults and larvae can be found in the soil.

Life Cycle and Detection

White grubs and billbugs damage the grass by feeding on the roots about an inch below the soil surface. Their feeding causes the grass to turn yellow and then brown. The damage may first appear as spots only a few inches in diameter, but these spots will gradually become larger as feeding continues. Heavy infestations completely destroy the roots, and the grass can be rolled back like a carpet.

Figure 34

Billbug larva.

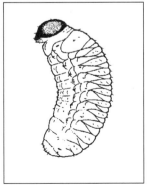

Moles, skunks, and armadillos feed on the grubs and may damage the lawn searching for them.

The Japanese beetle is the most important white grub pest. Adult female beetles lay their eggs in the soil in June and July and the grubs hatch and feed on grass roots. The most serious damage occurs in late August through October.

Inspect for grubs and billbugs by going to the edge of a damaged patch of grass and with your spade or knife, make cuts on three sides of a 12-inch square. Pry this flap back and examine the roots and upper 3 inches of soil for white grubs. Heavily infested patches can be lifted and rolled back like a throw rug. Count the number of grubs in this area. Move on to another patch and count the number of grubs you find. After sampling the edges of several dead or dying areas, determine the average number of grubs per square foot. As a rule of thumb, if an average of 5 to 7 grubs or 6 to 10 billbug larvae are found per sq. ft., an insecticide is warranted to save the lawn from further damage.

There are other factors, such as disease, nutritional imbalance, and drought, that will result in off-colored areas in lawns. Examine the lawn carefully to determine what corrective measures are needed.

Control

A biological approach to managing Japanese beetle grubs is with a microbial insecticide called milky spore disease (*Bacillus popilliae*). It is best applied in late summer or in the spring when the grubs are actively feeding on roots near the soil surface. The grubs become infected when they feed on the treated grass. When the grubs die, they release billions of spores back into the soil to infect future generations of grubs. Unfortunately, variable success has resulted in the use of this biological control.

If you choose to use chemical control, apply an insecticide when the grubs are small and feeding near the surface in late August and September. Billbug larvae can be treated when their threshold number of 6 to 10 billbug larvae per sq. ft. has been reached.

Apply the insecticide properly. Read and understand all directions on the container label regarding dosage rates, application information, and precautions. Most insecticides should be watered-in immediately with $^1/_2$ inch of water after application.

Disease Management

Diseases damage and thin-out lawns. Fortunately, diseases are less severe on properly managed lawns than grasses not receiving proper care. Because of costly pesticide applications, follow good cultural practices that will enhance the vigor of the grasses and increase their tolerance to diseases.

Fungi cause the most common and severe diseases of turfgrasses. Fungi are unique threadlike organisms that cannot produce their own food. They survive on dead or living plant and animal matter. Many fungi reproduce by forming spores, which are microscopic, seedlike bodies. Some spores may survive for long periods of time, until conditions favor disease development. They are spread by wind, water, mowers, and other equipment, and infected plant parts such as grass clippings. Fungi can also be introduced to a lawn through planting material, such as infected sprigs, plugs, or sod.

Just as humans are weakened from fatigue or malnutrition, making them more vulnerable to illnesses, turfgrasses stressed by environmental factors are more susceptible to infection by diseases. Drought-stressed turf is more susceptible to damage from diseases such as red thread and dollar spot. Mowing too short weakens turf and makes it susceptible to leaf spot. Fertilization is also an important factor in disease development. Dollar spot and red thread are more severe on nitrogen-deficient turf. Brown patch and Pythium blight are more severe on heavily fertilized turf.

Turfgrass species and cultivars vary in their susceptibility to diseases. It is important to grow those grasses that have the widest resistance to diseases.

Favorable Environmental Conditions

Light, temperature, and moisture not only influence the health of turfgrass plants and their ability to resist diseases, but also the growth of pathogens or disease-causing organisms. Moisture is necessary for the germination, infection, reproduction, and spread of disease-causing fungi. With a few exceptions, fungi are more damaging to turfgrass plants during wet weather or when dew or irrigation remains on the leaves for a long time.

Fungi also have specific temperature ranges within which they are active (Tables 17 and 18). The fungi that cause snow mold are active only during cold weather. Fungi that cause dollar spot and Pythium blight are most active during warm, humid weather. Some fungi contain species that are active under different temperature levels. Pythium blight and brown patch are caused by different species of *Pythium* or *Rhizoctonia* fungi that favor cool or warm temperatures.

Diagnosing Turfgrass Diseases

Fungal diseases are only one cause of turf loss. Treating for diseases will not lessen damage from other causes, such as insects or drought stress. Controlling turfgrass disease depends on accurate diagnosis. Disease management strategies that effectively combat one disease may have no effect on, and may even worsen, another disease.

Nature of Disease Symptoms

There are two types of disease symptoms to look for in a turfgrass area when you have a suspected disease problem. First, look at the entire turf area to identify any visible patterns such as a circular patch, spots, rings or circles. Sometimes disease symptoms do not show any type of pattern. For example, certain diseases will never appear as a ring, while others almost always do.

After examining the entire lawn, inspect individual plants in the affected area. Symptoms to look for on individual plants include leaf spots, leaf blighting, wilt, yellowing, stunting, and root rot. Leaf spots can be an important diagnostic clue as leaf spots of different diseases are usually unique in shape, size, and color. Also, examine the grass type that is affected and determine if surrounding weeds are affected. Noting the weather conditions will also help in making an accurate diagnosis because some diseases occur under certain conditions.

Signs of Disease

Signs of a disease are evidence of a pathogen causing the disease. The "green stuff" on moldy bread, for example, is the sign of a mold fungus. The fungi that cause most diseases are microscopic. But with stripe smut, powdery mildew and rust diseases, the spores of the disease-causing fungus pile up in such numbers they become visible on grass blades as black, white, or orange powder. With the disease red thread, the fungus sticks together and forms pink or red antler-like threads that grow from the leaf tips. This sign is a typical diagnostic feature of red thread. When the fungus can be seen, its appearance is often the most important clue for disease diagnosis. Some fungi are seen only in the early morning when dew is present or during periods of high moisture.

Environmental/Site Conditions

One of the most important factors used to forecast disease problems is the environmental condition at the turfgrass site. These conditions will also aid in diagnosing a disease. The weather plays an important role in disease development. Hot, humid weather is a perfect environment for brown patch development in tall fescue and other cool-season grasses, for instance. The physical and chemical properties of the soil and the surroundings are also important for diseases. These factors include soil drainage, air movement, amount of sun or shade, and closeness to other plantings or buildings. Prior applications of a pesticide or fertilizer can also influence disease development. The important thing to consider with turfgrass diseases is that these pests develop from an interaction of both cultural and environmental factors.

Disease Control Methods

Managing turfgrass diseases involves altering conditions to favor turfgrass growth and inhibit diseases. This includes using proper turfgrass management techniques and providing a good growing environment.

Management Practices

Proper management practices will help to reduce the amount of disease that will occur on your lawn. These practices include using recommended fertilization rates and applying them at the proper time, as well as proper mowing and watering practices. Applying too much fertilizer, especially nitrogen, will encourage disease development. Also, an improper balance of soil nutrients will weaken the turf, making it more susceptible to disease. Use soil testing to your advantage to reduce this problem.

When mowing, use a mower with a sharp blade and follow recommended height and frequency of cut.

Irrigate the soil deeply and infrequently, and water late at night after dewfall or during the early morning hours so the turf will not stay wet all night. Watering during the evening hours will only increase the chance of diseases occurring. If a thatch

layer exists, dethatch the lawn at the proper time.

Turfgrass diseases are easily managed when the turf is grown under proper environmental conditions. If the site is shady, establish a lawn grass that will tolerate the amount of shade present. Provide for good air circulation by selectively thinning out limbs or removing dense areas of vegetation around the site. If drainage is a problem, the soil may need to be internally drained using tile drain pipe placed in the soil. Improved air circulation and water drainage will also discourage weed development. Reducing thatch, increasing sunlight, regulating fertilizer applications, and proper mowing are all methods for reducing disease and ensuring a vigorous turf which will recover from disease damage. Basically, all cultural techniques that enhance deeper rooting will help strengthen the turf against disease attacks.

Resistant Cultivars

Seeding disease-resistant grasses is an excellent way to minimize turf loss from disease. When establishing new turf areas or renovating disease-damaged turf, select grasses resistant to the disease that damaged the existing stand and to diseases that are common in the area.

If a resistant cultivar of a particular grass species is not available, it may be possible to use another grass species that is resistant to common, local diseases. Disease severity can be reduced by changing the turfgrass being grown. It is a foolish practice to continue replanting the same grass that has been killed by the same disease year after year.

In selecting grasses for turf establishment or renovation, use mixtures of different grasses, or blends of varieties, rather than a single species. Using mixtures or blends produces a diverse population of grass plants that is often more successful in surviving stress and attack by disease. Make sure the mixture you select is suitable for your part of the state and the situations in which it will be used.

Diseases*

The following section describes common lawn diseases in South Carolina and includes causes, symptoms, and cultural or mechanical controls. For more detailed descriptions of turfgrass diseases, refer to the "References and Further Reading" section at the end of this chapter.

*Bruce Martin, Ph.D., "Turfgrass Diseases," *Southern Lawns.*

Figure 35

Brown patch on fescue.

Brown Patch or Large Patch

The term "brown patch" or Rhizoctonia blight, refers to a description of symptoms of diseases caused by a closely related group of fungi in the genus *Rhizoctonia*. Most cool- and warm-season lawn grasses are susceptible to brown patch. In fact, it is the most common and important patch disease of tall fescue in the Southeast (Figure 35). Cool-season grasses are attacked during warm, humid weather. Disease develops rapidly in cool-season grasses when nighttime temperatures equal or exceed 78 °F and there is high relative humidity. Severe infections result in death or thinning of lawn areas, creating opportunities for invading weeds.

Warm-season grasses, such as St. Augustinegrass, centipedegrass, bermudagrass, and zoysiagrass are also susceptible to large patch diseases (Figure 36). Most often it appears in the spring as the turfgrass emerges from dormancy or in the fall as the

Figure 36

Brown patch on centipedegrass.

turfgrass goes into dormancy. Infections sometimes occur in midwinter.

Symptoms

Individual diseased patches of turf may be several feet in diameter. Under drier conditions the affected areas may be smaller and appear sunken because diseased leaves have collapsed. Grass in the center of such patches may be unaffected or may recover more rapidly than grass at the margins. This results in ring or doughnut-shaped areas. Sometimes a circular patch is not evident. In such cases a large area may be thinned and eventually killed by the pathogen. This is often seen on St. Augustinegrass growing in moist, shady locations.

Examination of individual infected leaves reveals gray or tan irregular lesions with tan or brown borders. If conditions are only marginally favorable for disease development, only leaf lesions may develop. However, if conditions remain favorable for disease development, entire leaves may be consumed.

Control

Avoid high nitrogen fertilization especially during warm temperatures when cool-season grasses are under stress. In warm-season-grasses, avoid high nitrogen fertilization in the fall or spring when the disease is likely to appear. Several fungicides are labelled and provide good control especially when applied on a preventive schedule.

Figure 37

Dollar spot on bermuda.

Dollar Spot

Dollar spot (Figure 37) is a persistent disease on several turfgrasses. It occurs on fescue, bluegrass, and ryegrass. Susceptible warm-season species include bermudagrass, zoysiagrass, and occasionally

Table 17

Disease calender for warm-season grasses.

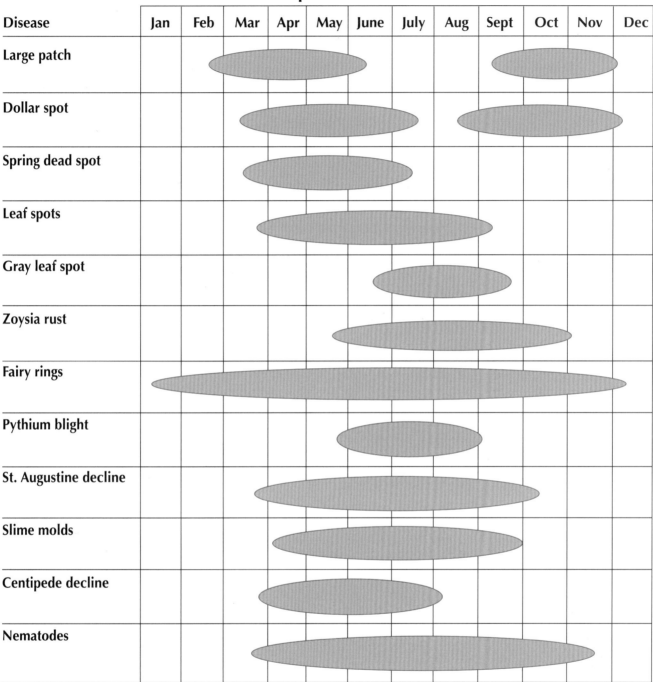

centipede and St. Augustinegrass. Dollar spot is favored by warm, humid weather and is more severe on nitrogen-deficient turf and in dry soils. High humidity in the turf canopy favors fungal growth. When dollar spot fungi are active, tufts of fungal growth in small spots are frequently seen in early morning hours. This sign of disease is easily confused with early stages of Pythium blight.

Symptoms

On closely mowed turf, small patches of about 1 to 2 in. in diameter develop. On higher cut turf, patches may exceed 5 or more inches in diameter. Individual diseased leaves of grasses exhibit characteristic lesions which are tan or bleached with distinct reddish-brown or purplish margins. Leaves may be girdled and collapse at the lesion even

Table 18

Disease calender for cool-season grasses.

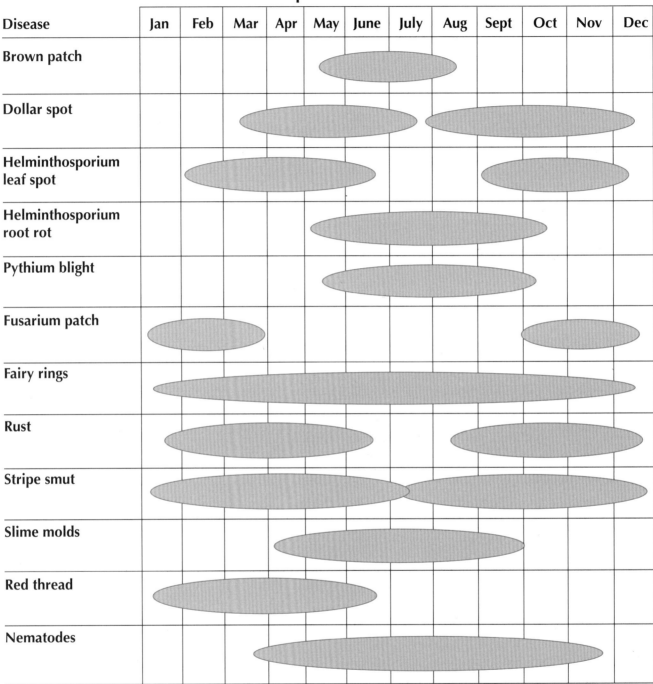

Expected Time of Disease Occurrence

Disease	Jan	Feb	Mar	Apr	May	June	July	Aug	Sept	Oct	Nov	Dec
Brown patch					X	X	X					
Dollar spot				X	X	X	X	X	X	X		
Helminthosporium leaf spot			X	X	X	X			X	X	X	
Helminthosporium root rot						X	X	X	X			
Pythium blight						X	X	X				
Fusarium patch	X	X									X	X
Fairy rings			X	X	X	X	X	X	X	X	X	X
Rust			X	X	X	X			X	X	X	X
Stripe smut			X	X	X	X	X	X	X	X	X	X
Slime molds				X	X	X	X	X				
Red thread			X	X	X	X						
Nematodes					X	X	X	X	X	X	X	X

though the leaf tips remain green. In contrast, lesions caused by *Pythium* fungi generally are water-soaked in appearance, feel greasy to the touch, or do not have distinct borders around the bleached diseased leaf tissue.

Control

Balanced fertility to avoid nitrogen deficiencies reduces disease severity. Irrigate during early morning hours to limit periods of high humidity and leaf wetness and promote air circulation. Mow regularly at the correct height of cut. Several fungicides provide good control but are generally unnecessary in home lawns.

Spring Dead Spot

Spring dead spot (Figure 38) is a serious disease of bermudagrass that occurs in areas where bermuda-grass undergoes complete dormancy in winter. Spring dead spot is common in the

Figure 38

Spring Dead Spot on bermuda.

Piedmont and Mountains, but is less common in Coastal regions.

Spring dead spot is more common on sterile hybrid cultivars of bermudagrass than on common seeded types. Generally, the disease appears in bermudagrass turfs that are 3 to 6 years of age. Excessive thatch, late summer nitrogen applications, and low temperatures in winter have been implicated as predisposing factors for spring dead spot development.

Symptoms

Dead circular areas of turf are present in the spring as the bermudagrass breaks dormancy. These patches may be 2 or 3 ft. in diameter. Commonly, the dead areas occur in circles with apparently healthy grass in the center, giving a "doughnut" appearance. The dead areas may persist over the summertime, with poor or weak colonization of patches by the stolons of healthy bermuda-grass. Patches of diseased turf may persist for several years and may gradually enlarge over years.

Control

Maintain a balanced fertilization program for bermudagrass, avoiding high rates of late-summer nitrogen applications. Avoid practices that increase thatch development, and aerify or dethatch areas where thatch has accumulated excessively. The previous practices serve to increase the chance of survival of low temperatures in winter. Some successful control with certain fungicides has been obtained when applications were made in September and October. Fungicide applications should only be considered after suggested cultural practices have been followed.

Gray Leaf Spot

Gray leaf spot is a common disease of St. Augustinegrass wherever it is grown. The disease occurs in very hot and humid weather conditions, generally being more severe in newly established turf areas, in shady locations, and locations with poor air movement. The fungus forms spores that are easily spread by wind and moisture or the activities of man.

Figure 39

Gray Leaf Spot on St. Augustine.

Symptoms

Infected leaves and stems have small, oblong, tan lesions with purple borders (Figure 39). The gray spores can sometimes be seen during warm, wet weather. When severe, the entire lawn may look scorched.

Control

Collect the infected clippings while mowing and compost them. During the growing season use moderate amounts of nitrogen fertilizer, preferably one that contains $^1/_4$ to $^1/_2$ of the nitrogen in a slow-release form. Improve air movement and light penetration in areas prone to chronic infections. Water during the early morning hours to promote maximum drying conditions during the day.

Fairy Rings

Fairy rings appear as rings or arcs of green, stimulated turf which may or may not be accompanied by adjacent areas of dead or declining grass (Figure 40 and Figure 41). Some of the fungi that are associated with fairy rings produce toxic substances which may accumulate in soil and actually kill turfgrass. More often, however, problems develop when mushroom mycelia accumulate in the soil and cause

Figure 40

Fairy Ring on bermudagrass.

Figure 41

Fairy Ring on centipedegrass.

the soil to become hydrophobic (hard to wet). The turfgrass comes under stress and declines because of a lack of water. Fairy rings may be very persistent in turf areas and tend to increase in diameter year after year. The fungi that cause fairy rings feed on old roots, stumps, or even thatch accumulations in the turf.

Control

Fairy rings are difficult to control. Measures that have shown limited success include tilling the area thoroughly and deeply. Sometimes, symptoms can be masked or toxins can be leached from the soil by prolonged irrigation to saturate the soil for several hours and over several days. If fairy rings are occurring consistently around trees over several growing seasons, it may be futile to attempt to eradicate the fungi. In this case, consider mulching underneath the trees or planting ground covers.

Pythium Blight

Pythium blight is a disease caused by several species of fungi in the genus *Pythium*. Warm-season grasses may also be affected by Pythium blight, but are generally less susceptible than cool-season grasses. All cool-season grasses are susceptible to Pythium blight. Pythium blight can be devastating to swards of ryegrass during hot (80 to 95 °F), wet or very humid weather, especially when air movement is limited. Young ryegrass or rough bluegrass plants used for overseeding are very susceptible in late summer or early fall. Large areas of turf can be damaged overnight.

Some *Pythium* species infect roots and crowns of cool-season grasses in winter or spring and cause stunting and yellowing. A root rot may result in a slow decline of turf areas. Poor surface and subsurface drainage favors development of *Pythium* fungi and encourages development of algae in areas where disease has weakened or killed the grass.

Symptoms

Round to irregular spots from an inch in diameter on closely mowed turf up to several inches in diameter on higher cut turfgrass suddenly appear. The leaves in affected spots appear water-soaked, slimy to the touch, and copper colored, dark brown or black when disease is active. As humidity and/or temperature decreases, spots appear straw-colored and lesions on leaves are tan, without a distinct border between diseased and green tissue. Generally, leaves in the centers of diseased patches or spots are completely blighted (without distinct lesions).

Control

Provide good surface and subsurface drainage. Remove shrubs, tree limbs, and other obstructions to increase air movement and light penetration to improve conditions commonly associated with chronic problems with Pythium blight or root rot. High nitrogen fertility also increases susceptibility to Pythium blight, thus a balanced fertility program will decrease susceptibility. Seed treatment with the fungicide mefeoxam has improved control of damping-off and seedling blight. When practical, it is suggested that one delay seeding cool-season grasses for overseeded areas to avoid high temperatures in late summer. When conditions favor disease development, fungicide applications provide good control.

Helminthosporium Diseases (Melting Out, Leafspot, Net-Blotch, Crown and Root Rot)

Several fungal species cause Helminthosporium diseases. They survive in dead tissue, thatch, or soil as spores and dormant mycelium. Films of moisture must be present on leaf tissues for spore germination and infection. Thus, these diseases are favored by prolonged periods of wet or humid weather. Improper irrigation practices also provide infection periods of longer duration. Centipedegrass is rarely adversely affected by these fungi.

Symptoms

Gradual browning and thinning occurs over a period of weeks or months. As disease progresses, larger irregular areas turn yellow, then brown and thin out. Some warm-season grasses, such as bermudagrass, may develop irregular patches or thinning of large areas. On bermudagrass or zoysiagrass, small linear brown lesions appear on leaf blades and sheaths in spring or fall and may expand to larger irregular lesions with tan, white, or straw-colored centers.

Drechslera species cause leaf spots during cool, humid conditions, with crown and root phases occurring in warm, dry weather or during wet periods following dry periods. *Drechslera* species occur mostly on cool-season grasses. Symptoms vary on different turfgrasses but generally, leaf lesions are distinct and begin as tiny water-soaked areas that become dark brown to purplish black. These lesions are usually surrounded by a yellow area of varying width that fades to the normal green of the leaf tissue. Older lesions may have a white or bleached area in the center of the lesion. Severely affected plants may become almost entirely yellow in appearance.

Control

Avoid high nitrogen fertilization and watering practices that provide long periods of wet or humid conditions. Frequent mowing at proper heights will provide better drying conditions in the turf canopy and help reduce the leaf spot phases of these diseases. Provide adequate water during infrequent but deep irrigation to help avoid crown and root rot phases.

Resistance is being incorporated into many varieties of perennial ryegrasses and red fescues. Also, the common use of blends of different varieties of turfgrasses used in lawns or overseeded areas should limit the development of major epidemics. However, fungicides are necessary for high maintenance turf areas.

Nematode Management

In many sandy soil areas of the Southeast, nematodes are among the most important and least well understood of those pests. Nematode damage to turf is more common in the South than in most other places. Sandy soils, drought conditions and a long growing season favor development of very high nematode populations and also create conditions in which grasses are especially sensitive to their effects.

Morphology

Nematodes are tiny, unsegmented roundworms, generally transparent and colorless. Most are slender, with bodies from $1/100$ to $1/8$ inch long. They are essentially invisible to the unaided eye.

Life Cycle and Reproduction

Plant parasitic nematodes have a fairly simple life cycle which has six stages: the egg, four juvenile stages, and adult. Inside the egg, the embryo develops into the first stage juvenile. The first stage juvenile molts inside the eggshell to become a second-stage juvenile, which hatches from the egg, and in most species, must feed before continuing to develop. The nematode molts three more times to become a fully developed adult.

Male and female nematodes occur in most species, and both may be required for reproduction. Reproduction without males is common, however, and some species are hermaphroditic ("females" produce both sperms and eggs). With the production of eggs by the individual, the cycle is complete. The length of the life cycle varies considerably with each species, its host plant, and the temperature of its habitat. Rates of activity, growth, and reproduction increase as soil temperature rises, from about 50 °F to about 90 °F. Minimum generation time is about 4 weeks for many nematodes under optimum conditions (about 81 °F for many nematodes)

The number of eggs deposited by a female varies among species and is affected by the habitat. Most species produce between 50 and 500 eggs, but a few sometimes produce several thousand eggs per female. Eggs of some species can survive without hatching for years but hatch quickly when a host plant grows near them.

Where Nematodes Live and How They Affect Plants

Plant nematodes are aquatic animals that live in soil water or in plant fluids. They are obligate parasites that must feed on living plant tissues to survive. All have some form of hollow oral stylet or spear, much like a hypodermic needle, which is used to puncture the host cell wall. Many (probably all) plant nematodes inject enzymes into the host cell before feeding. These enzymes partially digest the cell contents before they are sucked into the gut. Most of the injury that nematodes cause to plants is related in some way to this feeding process.

Root galling is caused by growth-regulating chemicals in the saliva of some nematodes. Feeding of others stops growth of roots, causing stubby, swollen root tips and lateral root proliferation. As they move through roots, endoparasitic nematodes can cause open wounds which allow rot and wilt disease organisms to invade them. The wounds and other effects of feeding often cause physiological changes in plants, making them more susceptible to many plant diseases, sometimes even breaking plant resistance to diseases. Some plant nematodes can store and transmit some plant viruses. Nematodes may feed on plant tissue from outside the plant (*ectoparasitic*) or inside the tissue (*endoparasitic*). If the adult females move freely through the soil or plant tissue, that nematode species is said to be migratory. Those species in which the adult females become permanently immobile in one place in a root are termed sedentary.

Ectoparasitic nematodes are nearly all migratory or mobile. Most feed superficially at or very near the root tip or on root-hairs, although a few have stylets long enough to reach several cells deep (Figure 42). The ectoparasites which cause the most widespread and severe turf injury are the sting (*Belonolaimus* spp.), stubby root (*Trichodorus* and related species), and awl (*Dolichodorus* spp.) nematodes. These feed at or near root tips and usually inhibit root elongation.

Turfgrass Nematodes

Many kinds of nematodes damage turf; their feeding may alter root growth, cause small dead spots in the soft root tissues, or even kill the roots. Fungi often cause extensive rot of roots which have been injured by nematodes, and turf weakened by nematodes may be more susceptible to many kinds of diseases.

Figure 42

Ectoparasitic nematodes feed superficially on root tissue.

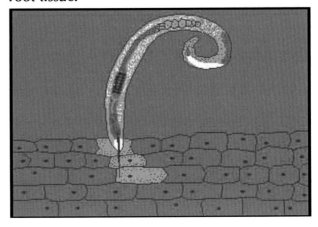

Nematodes important as turf pests are described briefly below, with indications of the lowest numbers of each kind of nematode expected to cause significant damage. Properly maintained turf can often stand much higher populations than the minimal action levels cited (AL = number of nematodes/100 cc. soil).

Sting Nematode

Sting nematode (*Belonolaimus longicaudatus*) damages all grasses commonly grown in the Southeast although bahiagrass is somewhat tolerant. Generally, they are only found in very sandy soils. Where conditions favor this nematode, it is the most damaging nematode pest of lawn grasses (AL = 10).

Lance Nematode

Lance nematodes (*Hoplolaimus* spp.) is a common turf pest because they attack all commonly-grown grasses, are easily distributed with sod and sprigs, and adapt readily to many soil conditions. They are the most important nematode pest of St. Augustinegrass (AL = 40).

Ring Nematode

Ring nematodes (*Criconemella* spp. and relatives) have a wide distribution. They are found on all turfgrasses but are considered a major pest only on centipedegrass. If populations are high enough, they can damage bermudagrass and zoysiagrass (AL = 150 for centipedegrass; 500 for most others).

Root-knot Nematode

Root-knot nematodes (*Meloidogyne* spp.) are widely distributed, found most frequently in St. Augustinegrass, zoysiagrass, and bermudagrass. The effects of these nematodes on turf are not well known, but they are believed to be injurious at high population densities (AL = 80).

Stubby-root Nematode

Stubby-root nematodes (*Paratrichodorus* spp. and related genera) live in most soils in the Coastal Plain; damage is similar to sting nematodes (AL = 40).

Diagnosing Damage

Plant parasitic nematodes (alone and especially in combination with other stresses related to drought, nutritional status and fungal diseases) can cause serious damage to lawns. Symptoms of nematode damage to turfgrasses can be easily confused with the effects of nutritional deficiencies, water or heat stress, or other diseases. Do not depend on symptoms alone when trying to tell if nematodes are damaging turf, since may other factors can cause similar symptoms. A good diagnosis should be based on most or all of the symptoms above and below ground, lawn history, and laboratory assay of soil and/or root samples.

Plant-parasitic nematodes damage plants directly by their feeding activities which involve puncturing cells (mostly in the root system) with the needlelike stylet in the head, injecting digestive juices into the cells, and then sucking the liquid contents out. Uptake of nutrients and water by the roots is adversely affected. Since the nematodes mostly damage turfgrass roots, symptoms of injury often go unnoticed until soil water is limiting. These symptoms are often confused with environmental stress symptoms or nutritional problems and may be difficult to diagnose. Extended growing season, warm climate, and sandy soils favor development of very high nematode populations and also create conditions in which grasses are most susceptible to nematode damage. Diagnosing nematode problems is often difficult, but there are several clues that help. These include the type of symptoms, pattern and timing of damage, previous history, nematode species present and the results of nematode counts.

Above-Ground Symptoms

Symptoms appear as wilting, thinning or gradual decline, yellowing of leaves but without lesions or deformities (Figure 43). Again, these symptoms are not unique to nematodes and can be caused by heat or drought stresses, nutrient deficiency, fungal

diseases, insect feeding, soil compaction, prolonged saturation of soil with water, or chemical contamination.

Since most plant parasitic nematodes affect roots, most above-ground symptoms are the result of inadequate water supply or mineral nutrition, including wilting under moderate moisture stress, slow recovery of wilted areas after rain or irrigation, and thinning of the turf canopy. The turfgrass is weakened by the nematode damage and is unable to outcompete invading weeds, such as sedges, spurges, and Florida pusley.

Root Symptoms

Root systems injured by nematodes are usually dark, short, and lack normal lateral or "feeder" roots (Figure 44). Some nematodes feed on root tips, and induce a short, excessively hairy-appearing root system. These symptoms are typical of damage by sting, awl or high populations of stubby root nematodes. Some nematodes induce swellings, root lesions, and stubby swollen root tips. The result is accelerated rotting or blackening of roots and proneness of plants to wilting. Heavily affected root systems have much less soil clinging to them when a plug is pulled from the turf compared to unaffected turfgrass stands. The root symptoms, however, are not unique to nematodes and should always be considered in conjunction with other observations when diagnosing nematode problems.

Patterns of Damage

Nematode populations are unevenly distributed in soil, so great variation in numbers encountered within a few feet are very common. Nematode move-

Figure 43

Healthy bermudagrass (left) compared to sting nematode-infested bermudagrass (right).

Figure 44

Sting nematode damage to bermudagrass roots (left) compared to normal roots (right).

Credit: Bob Dunn.

ment in soil is very slow, when they move on their own. In undisturbed turf, visible symptoms may appear as round, oval, or irregularly lobed areas which gradually increase in size. Nematode damage is often seen first and most pronounced in areas under stress from traffic, excessive drainage (slopes or sandy soils), or areas outside the perimeter of irrigation. The boundary of damaged areas is generally diffuse, not an abrupt change from damaged to healthy turf.

Timing of Damage

Plant parasitic nematodes are obligate parasites and feed most when the turfgrass roots are actively growing. They are therefore most numerous during mild weather, in early summer (May-June) and early fall (October-November) on warm-season grasses, and mid to late spring and again in fall on cool-season grasses. The turf usually shows no above-ground symptoms of nematode damage until unfavorable environmental conditions prevail. For example, expect to see nematode injury during hot, dry periods when water in the soil is not in adequate supply to support both the turf and nematode needs.

Previous History

The history of an area is important information. Specific nematode, disease and insect problems identified in the past may suggest pests likely to be affecting lawn grasses in the present. If a particular nematode pest was determined to be present at significant numbers in the past, it is likely the nematodes will continue to be a problem.

Soil Sampling

Soil assay for nematode identification and relative numbers of particular nematodes are the surest way to determine whether a problem in the turf is indeed caused by parasitic nematodes. It is good practice to take soil and root samples periodically so that changes in the populations of plant parasitic nematodes in the turfgrass stand could be monitored. Given the irregular distribution of nematodes in the soil, it is important that adequate soil/root sampling be conducted in order to confirm the nematode.

Sampling Procedures

1. Most nematodes are in the root zone and samples should be taken to represent that area. Samples should be taken from both poor-growing and healthy appearing plants.
2. Take samples when soil is moist but not wet. A single sample should be made up of 10 to 20 small samples from symptomatic vs. nonsymptomtic areas. The composite sample should be one quart of soil. A good procedure is to use a 1-inch core sampler. If that is not available, use a shovel to cut through the soil profile and then take a 1 to 2 in. slice from the edge of the opening to simulate a soil core.
3. Sample turf sites in a zigzag pattern from 3 to 5 in. deep. If there are dead or dying areas, take the sample from the interface of the good and poor areas.
4. Place the mixed sample in a sealed plastic bag, labeled with your name and sample number. Label the outside of the bag with location information using a permanent marker. Fill out the submission form as completely as possible. Accurate information helps the diagnosticians do a better job for you.
5. Keep samples cool, below 80 °F if practical, and out of direct sunlight. Do not put samples in the back of trucks, trunks or in non-insulated floorboards of vehicles. Take the samples to your county Clemson Extension office.

Damage Thresholds

The relative importance of many nematodes to the various grasses has been established through many years of experience and experimentation. Action levels are based on the numbers of particular nematodes per 100 cc. of soil. However, these action levels should be taken as a guideline only, because the effects of cultural practices and turf vigor on nematode damage. There is also a wide variation in how much injury is acceptable, depending on the grass, personal aesthetic standards, and maintenance budget. Be aware that threshold numbers from different laboratories may differ. Clemson University has established thresholds that are published in *Nematode Guidelines for South Carolina*, Clemson Extension Circular 703.

Both private and university laboratories provide good nematode assay. It is usually best to work with one lab since assay methods and results may differ between laboratories.

Managing Nematodes

Currently, no synthetic pesticide is available to treat residential turf to reduce nematode damage. Therefore, to a great extent, managing nematodes in home lawns must depend on sound cultural practices and nematode-tolerant grasses.

Cultural practices

Cultural practices help minimize stresses that make the turfgrass more susceptible to nematodes. To facilitate deeper penetration of the soil by roots, irrigate deeply and less frequently instead of shallow, daily watering. However, in sandy soils with significant nematode infestations may require more frequent irrigation to compensate for the soil conditions and damaged root system. To achieve proper infiltration and adequate oxygen levels in the soil, coring with narrow, hollow tines or spiking should be performed in late spring and early summer. Cultivation should be performed at times of the year when best turf recovery occurs: in late spring and early summer for warm-season turfgrasses and in mid-spring or early fall for cool-season turfgrasses.

Excessive fertilization with water-soluble nitrogen should be avoided since nematode numbers increase rapidly on succulent roots and, during periods of environmental stress, especially in summer, the roots are placed under additional strain. Organic forms of nitrogen have been shown to be associated with lower nematode numbers than inorganic forms. However, judicious use of a balanced fertilizer is always advocated. Plant diseases, nutrient deficiencies, and soil compaction should be managed or minimized in order to decrease the impact of nematode diseases on in lawns. Avoid mowing too low to prevent additional stress.

Adding organic matter to improve soil structure and moisture retention in sandy soils will help improve the growing environment for the grasses. At the same time, it creates a favorable environment for the growth of natural predators of the nematode.

Use tolerant grasses

Whenever possible, avoid planting species or cultivars that are the most susceptible to the nematode species deemed problematic in a given locality. Sometimes nematode damage is worse because a poorly adapted grass has been established at the particular site. If turf must be replaced because of nematodes, the new turf usually will become established faster if the number of nematodes can be reduced prior to planting.

Bahiagrasses generally tolerate nematodes better than other common grasses and are less likely to have high nematode populations. Sting nematodes may injure bahiagrasses, but sheath nematodes rarely affect it. However, bahiagrass may not provide acceptable lawn quality.

Bermudagrasses may be severely damaged by sting, lance, stubby root and some other nematodes. Low mowing and high maintenance requirements for many bermudagrasses often increase their susceptibility to nematode injury.

Centipedegrass is very susceptible to ring, sting, sheath and stubby root nematodes. Some problems are encountered with centipedegrass in sandy coastal soils with a high native soil pH due to calcium carbonate from sea shells. Centipedegrass is poorly adapted to these sites, and ring nematodes take advantage of the weakened turf. Other grasses better adapted should perform better in these sites.

St. Augustinegrass is susceptible to sting and to lance nematodes, especially if overfertilized and over-watered. Other nematodes are usually less damaging.

Zoysiagrasses are susceptible to most nematodes that injure other turfgrasses. Sting nematodes injury zoysia severely, and root knot nematodes are frequently encountered on zoysia more than other warm season grasses.

Biological Controls

There are several products on the market for managing plant parasitic nematodes using a variety of natural products. For instance, mixtures of chitin from seashells and urea have been shown to suppress root knot nematodes when the material is incorporated into soil. Another product utilizes preparations of sesame, which has been shown to be toxic to nematodes under some circumstances. Also, various bacteria have been shown to suppress nematodes and various commercial preparations of bacteria or bacterial products have come on the market. Although many of these materials may suppress nematodes for short periods of time, none have given results in the field to date that compares with the efficacy of chemical nematocides. Unfortunately, there is no effective chemical nematicide that is currently available for use on the home lawn.

Summary

Many kinds of nematodes can damage turf. Although their effects can easily be mistaken for those caused by many other problems, their diagnosis is possible by combined evidence from symptoms, history of the site, and laboratory analysis of soil samples. Chemical control options are not available for home lawn use and effective biological controls are not yet available. The best approach to minimizing nematode problems on your lawn is to manage your lawn properly to keep it healthy.

Organic Lawn Care

The "organic" approach to lawn care relies on the principles and techniques discussed in previous sections of this chapter. As with conventional lawn care, each maintenance practice influences another. When and how much you fertilize affects how often you mow. Your mowing height affects how often you need to water and how many weeds you have. However, unlike conventional lawn care which involves synthetic fertilizers and pesticides, organic lawn care uses organic or naturally derived products to fertilize the lawn and cultural and biological techniques to manage pests. This natural approach has the added long-term benefit of building healthy soil, which creates favorable growing conditions for the turfgrass and the soil dwelling inhabitants.

"Organic" is technically defined as carbon-containing or carbon-composed compounds. Most products used in lawn care contain carbon, thus, are organic. However, in the broad sense, "organic" is often associated with "natural" or "naturally derived" products or those products not grown with "synthetic" inputs.

The main theme of organic lawn care is working with nature to create a healthy, well-managed lawn which can resist invasion from weeds and attacks from insects and diseases. Organic lawn care is a similar approach as preventive health care. Prevent problems from occurring to avoid having to treat them. The following steps will help you establish and maintain a healthy, attractive organic lawn:

1. **Develop healthy soil.** Good soil is the foundation for a healthy lawn. Before establishing a lawn, add organic matter such as compost, composted pine bark, or peat moss. Organic matter improves drainage in clay soils and water retention in sandy soils. It also improves soil structure, which benefits the lawn and the beneficial earthworms and microbes that break down the organic matter to make the nutrients available to the grass plants.

Add organic matter to established lawns by topdressing or adding a shallow, one-quarter inch layer of compost. Topdress cool-season lawns in the fall and warm-season lawns in late spring after they emerge from dormancy.

2. **Choose grasses adapted to your region and your management style.** Select lawn grasses adapted to the soil and climatic conditions in your region and tolerate or resist pests. As described in other sections of this book, grasses differ in their appearance, adaptation, and ability to tolerate diseases and insects.

3. **Feed your lawn with organic fertilizers derived from natural organic sources.**

Organic fertilizers are derived from naturally occurring sources, usually waste or by-products of some type of processing such as composted animal manure, cottonseed meal, bloodmeal, and many others (Table 19). Although they contain relatively low concentrations of actual nutrients (usually between 2 and 10% nitrogen) compared to synthetic fertilizers, they increase the organic matter content of the soil and improve soil structure. Be careful with some organic fertilizers to ensure they do not contain weed seeds and excessive nitrate or urea are not present as with poultry manure which can burn the lawn.

Natural organic fertilizers rely on soil microorganisms to slowly break down the materials and release the nutrients. Several weeks or longer may be required for the nutrients to become available to the grass plants. Extended dry periods or cold temperatures may hamper the activity of microorganisms, thereby delaying the release of nitrogen from organic fertilizers. Before fertilizing your lawn, have your soil tested every two or three years through your Clemson Extension Service. Maintain the appropriate soil pH for your lawn grasses and select fertilizers that will apply minerals that are deficient in the soil. Microbial activity and the release of nutrients will be enhanced with a soil pH between 6 and 6.5 (5.8 for centipede- and carpetgrass), adequate moisture and oxygen, and temperatures above 50 to 55 °F.

4. Mow properly. Follow these basic rules of proper mowing to maintain a healthy, dense lawn:

- **Mow with a sharp mower blade.** Sharp blades cut the grass cleanly, ensuring rapid healing and regrowth. When dull blades tear and bruise the leaves, the wounded grass plants become weakened, appear ragged, and are less able to ward off invading weeds or to recover from disease or insect attacks.

- **Mow your lawn regularly, and only when the grass is dry.** A good rule-of-thumb is to remove no more than $^1/_3$ of the grass height at any one mowing. For example, if you are maintaining your centipedegrass lawn at $1^1/_2$ inches, mow the lawn when it is about 2 inches high. Following the $^1/_3$ rule will produce smaller clippings which will disappear quickly by filtering down to the soil surface.

- **Mow your lawn at the proper height.** By maintaining the appropriate height, you will create a dense lawn that can outcompete weeds for sunlight, water, and nutrients. In the summer, gradually raise the mowing height by $^1/_4$ to $^1/_2$ inch. A higher mowing height encourages deeper root growth and greater access to water and nutrients. Also, the added height enables the grass plants to block out competing weeds and to shade the soil to conserve moisture. Refer to the section on "Mowing" for suggested lawn mowing practices.

- **"Recycle" your grass clippings as you mow.** Returning your grass clippings to the lawn saves time, energy, and money. Besides, when you recycle grass clippings, you're also fertilizing the lawn by returning the nutritious grass clippings back to the soil. Contrary to popular belief, grass clippings will not contribute to the development of a thatch layer. As fresh clippings decompose, they improve the environment for earthworms and other soil dwelling thatch-decomposers.

5. Water wisely. Water only when the lawn really needs, especially if reseeding or resodding is not an option. As described in the "Irrigating" section, irrigate your lawn when it show signs of moisture stress: bluish-gray color; footprints that remain in the lawn after walking on it; and wilted, folded, or curled leaves. Water deeply: irrigate with $^3/_4$ to 1 inch of water when the grass shows signs of drought stress. Deep watering encourages deeper roots and stronger plants.

6. Core aerate or aerify compacted soils. Soil compaction occurs when soil particles in the top 4 inches of soil are compressed, reducing the pore spaces between them and impeding the movement of air, water, and nutrients to the grass roots. This, in turn, stresses the grass plants, making them less able to compete with weeds and slows recovery from injury. In time, a compacted lawn needs renovation.

Compaction is likely to be a problem in high-traffic spots. Sandy soils are less likely to become compacted than those comprised of clay and silt. Whenever heavy equipment rolls repeatedly over an existent or soon-to-be lawn area, especially when it's wet, the soil gets compressed and becomes compacted. See "Aerifying" on p. 36 for more information on alleviating compaction.

7. Correct thatch buildups. Thatch causes problems when it exceeds one-half inch in thickness. The grass develops roots within the thatch layer where it's unable to obtain adequate moisture and minerals. It also provides a habitat for destructive insects and disease-causing organisms.

8. Work with nature to manage pests. A healthy, organic lawn is likely to have some weeds or insect pests, but it will also have beneficial insects and other organisms that help keep pests under control. Maintain a strong healthy lawn to help it ward off weed invasions or cope with insects or diseases. When pest problems need attention, use cultural and biological controls to manage them.

Weeds. The best form of weed control is prevention. Follow good cultural practices that favor the growth and development of the lawn. Simply mowing your lawn with a sharp blade at the recommended height and frequency will help lawns fight weeds naturally.

When weeds occur, figure out what sparked the invasion. If the basic cause is not corrected, weeds

Table 19

Some organic fertilizer sources.

Nutrient	Product	Source(s)	Comments
Nitrogen	Natural organic fertilizers	Municipal sludge, composted poultry litter, animal proteins, bone meal, wheat germ, manure	Most contain a complete N-P-K ratio, but N rates are low (2 to 10%); some also supply micronutrients.
		Seaweed, kelp extracts	Source of N, Fe, and some micronutrients; often mixed with organic matter sources to encourage rooting and stress resistance.
Phosphorous	Bone meal	Pulverized poultry bones	More readily available P; dust; often hard to apply.
	Colloidal phosphate	Mine industry by-product	Contains 0-20-0. Slow-acting, long-lasting.
	Rock phosphate	Mining	Contains 0-33-0. Slow-acting, long-lasting.
Potassium	Wood ash	Fire places	Contains up to 4% elemental K; also a source of lime to raise soil pH.
	Sul-Po-Mag	Mining	Available as 0-0-21. Fast-acting, high burn potential.
	Granite dust	Mining by-product	Contain 0-0-5. Slow acting, long-lasting.
	Greensand	Mining	Contains 0-1-6. Slow-acting, long-lasting.
	Compost	Home and lawn trimmings	Contains up to 1% elemental K.
Iron	Humates	Mined extractions	Sources of various nutrients including iron.

will continue to occur despite attempts at trying to rid them. Weeds often appear as a result of poor management, such as improper mowing, watering, or fertilizing. Other factors that can indirectly lead to weed outbreaks by creating a weak or thin stand of grass are insects, diseases, compacted soil, and thatch.

Although time-consuming, handpull weeds when the soil is moist. For perennial weeds that come back year after year from underground plants parts, remove as much of the root system as possible because the remaining pieces of rhizomes or roots will develop into new plants.

If you choose to use a herbicide to nonselectively spot-treat or trim areas with weeds, consider an organic nonselective postemergent herbicide containing potassium salts of fatty acids (e.g., Sharp-Shooter®).

A preemergence herbicide containing corn gluten meal inhibits root development in certain germinating weed seeds. This yellow powder, which is a by-product of the wet milling process, has long been used as an additive to animal feed. Corn gluten meal is available as a herbicide under a variety of trade names (Safe 'n Simple® [Blue Seal Feeds] and Concern Weed Prevention Plus® [Necessary Organics, Inc.]). It's labeled as a preemergent herbicide for use on turfgrass, field crops, and home gardens. Among the weeds controlled by corn gluten meal are crabgrass, dandelions, smartweed, redroot pigweed, purslane, lamb's-quarters, foxtail, and barnyardgrass. Both powdered and pelleted forms are available.

Table 20

Selected organic insect control products.

Product	Insects Controlled	Comments
Resistant varieties of grass - 'Floratam' St. Augustinegrass	Chinch bugs	Limited available varieties.
Endophyte-enhanced cultivars (*Neotyphodium lolli, N. coenophialum, N. typhinum, Epichloe typhina*)	Armyworms, cutworms, billbugs, chinch bugs, sod webworms	Only active on leaf-feeding insects; available only in cool- season turfgrasses (tall fescue, perennial ryegrass).
Bacillus thuringiensis (Bt) bacteria	Armyworms, cutworms, sod webworms	Slow-acting, narrow spectrum of insects affected; not always effective.
Bacillus popilliae (Milky spore) bacteria	White grubs	Limited availability; inconsistent results.
Beauveria bassiana (fungus); *Metarhizium anisopliae* (fungus)	Chinch bugs, mole crickets, caterpillars, white grubs	Naturally-occurring cuticle disrupter, limited commercial production; inconsistent results.
Spinosad® (*Saccharopolyspora spinosa*)	Armyworms, cutworms, sod webworms	Only for leaf feeding insects.
Parasitic Wasps (*Ormia depleta*)	Mole crickets	Cold sensitive; not yet available.
Clamshell pieces (Clandosan®)	Armyworms, cutworms, nematodes	Limited availability; unproven.
Entomogenous nematodes (*Steinernema carpocapsae, S. glaseri, Heterorhabditis bacteriophora*)	Armyworms, cutworms, billbugs, white grubs, fleas, mole crickets, sod webworms, sod webworms	Numerous products for various pests; dependent on environmental conditions
Insecticidal soaps and oils	Armyworms, cutworms, sod webworms	Only soaps are used in turfgrass; effective on some caterpillars.
Azadirachtin (neem seed extract)	Armyworms, cutworms, sod webworms	Growth regulators used on small worms.
Diatomaceous earth	Armyworms, cutworms	Acts as a desiccant; effectiveness is reduced in moist conditions.
Traps	White grub adults	Various traps available for adult stages of Japanese beetles); however, results are unproven.

Timing is very important to achieve the best control. Corn gluten meal must be applied just prior to weed seed germination. If applied too early, soil microbes will limit its effect. Similarly, if the herbicide is applied too late there will be little reduction of root growth.

Corn gluten meal is most effective at controlling weed emergence during periods of drought. When there is abundant soil moisture, many of the weeds survive despite their stunted root systems. Nevertheless, research indicates up to 80% control of weeds over a three-year period.

Synthetic herbicides can provide 100% control. Corn gluten meal herbicide, which contains 10% nitrogen by weight, must be applied at a higher rate than conventional "weed-and-feed" herbicides.

This translates to as much as a threefold increase in cost per square foot. Nevertheless, you can experiment with this organic herbicide by trying it on small areas to see if you're pleased with the results.

Insects. Lawn grasses can be attacked by a variety of insects. By maintaining your lawn properly, you can reduce the susceptibility of your lawn to insect pests and allow it to tolerate more damage from their feeding. This includes proper fertilization, watering, mowing, and thatch control. Organic, slow-release fertilizers are a good choice because they do not increase the succulence of the turf like fast- release synthetic fertilizers, which make the grass more attractive to some insects.

Follow an IPM approach to manage insect pests. The first step is to grow an adapted, competitive grass. Next, monitor your lawn frequently for signs of insect damage. If a damaging insect is suspected, make a proper diagnosis, and, if needed, take appropriate action. Early detection and control will lessen the chance of losing a large amount of lawn. An organic approach to controlling turfgrass insects includes botanical pesticides and microbials (Table 20).

Botanical pesticides or botanicals are naturally occurring pesticides derived from plants. Two common botanicals include pyrethrins, insecticidal chemicals extracted from the pyrethrum flower (*Tanacetum cinerariifolium*), and neem, a botanical insecticide and fungicide extracted from the tropical neem tree (*Azadirachta indica*) that contains the active ingredient azadirachtin.

Microbial insecticides combat damaging insects with microscopic living organisms such as viruses, bacteria, fungi, protozoa, or nematodes. Although they may look like out-of-the-ordinary insecticides, they can be applied in ordinary ways—as sprays, dusts, or granules. The naturally occurring bacteria (*Bacillus popilliae*) that primarily infects Japanese beetle grubs, is a popular pathogen sold as Milky Spore Powder Japanese Beetle & Grub Control® as a long-term biological approach for managing Japanese beetle grubs. However, milky spore has been, at best, only marginally effective in the South.

Parasitic nematodes (*Steinernema carpocapsae*) have proven to be quite effective against adult and very large mole cricket nymphs. However, as biological control agents and living organisms, they need to be handled carefully and according to manufacturer's instructions to ensure their survival.

In recent years plant breeders have been working on varieties of lawn grasses that have insect resistance. This was accomplished by introducing a fungus (endophyte) into the grass plant which produces a chemical toxic to insects. Fine fescues with insect resistance include SR3000 and Jamestown II. Insect-resistant tall fescues include Arid, Mesa, Titan, and Tribute. Because the toxin does not move to underground plant parts, this insect resistance is limited to surface feeders such as sod webworms and chinch bugs.

Diseases. Proper management practices will help reduce the amount of disease that will occur on your lawn. Reducing thatch, increasing sunlight, fertilizing with appropriate amounts at the right times of year, watering the soil deeply and infrequently and late at night or early in the morning when dew has formed, and mowing properly are all methods for reducing disease and ensuring a vigorous lawn which will recover from disease injury.

Grow disease-resistant grasses to reduce the chances for disease outbreaks. When possible, use a blend of 3 or more varieties to take advantage of the varying levels of disease resistance in each one.

A lawn managed organically favors the management of a rich, healthy soil harbors huge populations of antagonistic microorganisms toward plant pathogens, including those that cause lawn diseases. Well-aged compost has been shown by researchers to contain disease- suppressing organisms. These microorganisms in the compost starve the plant pathogens by feeding on nutrients that would otherwise support the growth and spread of the fungal diseases.

Recently, several commercial fungicides have become available where their active ingredients were derived from various wood-decaying fungi. They include Heritage® (azoxystrobin) and Compass® (trifloxystrobin). These fungicides help control brown patch, pythium blight, snow mold, leaf spot, rust, take-all patch and some fairy rings. Although not organic in composition, a mixture of copper and sulfur, called Bordeaux mixture, has long been a fungicide for certain diseases in specific crops.

9. Set realistic goals for your lawn. Be realistic about the level of lawn quality desired and the amount of time or money available to spend to achieve that look. Do not attempt to attain a perfect golf course putting green quality lawn. A healthy lawn is likely to have some weeds or insect pests, but it will also have beneficial insects and other organisms that help keep pests under control. ❧

References and Further Reading

Southern Lawns; Best Management Practices for the Selection, Establishment, and Maintenance of Southern Lawngrasses. 2003. L. B. McCarty, ed. Clemson Extension Circ. 707, Clemson University Public Service Publishing, Clemson, SC.

Diseases of Turfgrasses in the Southeast. 1994. Bruce Martin. Clemson University Cooperative Extension Service Pub. EB 146.

Color Atlas of Turfgrass Weeds (2nd ed). 2008. L. B. McCarty, J. W. Everest, D. W. Hall, T. R. Murphy, F. Yelverton. Wiley and Sons. Wiley.com.

Internet

Clemson University Turfgrass Program Home Page: http://virtual.clemson.edu/groups/turfornamental/

Clemson University Home and Garden Information Center: http://hgic.clemson.edu

Clemson University Pesticide Information Program: http://entweb.clemson.edu/pesticid/saftyed/homeuse.htm

Ideally, test your soil before you fertilize to determine the soil pH and level of nutrients present in the soil. It can be done at anytime of year. Soil testing allows you to customize your fertilizer and lime applications to your plants' needs. It will also help prevent problems with nutrient deficiencies (in the case of under-fertilization) or problems associated with over-fertilization, such as excessive vegetative growth, delayed maturity, salt burn, and wasted money.

In addition, it can protect against any environmental hazards resulting from excessive fertilizer applications leading to leaching and runoff.

For an accurate test, collect a representative sample, which means collecting 12 or more cores and combining them into one composite sample. The samples should include soil from the surface to a depth of 6 to 8 inches in all areas except for lawns where cores should be taken from a depth of only 3 to 6 inches.

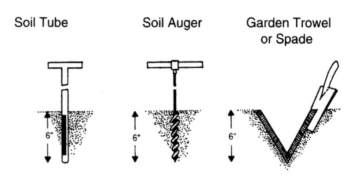

Use a soil auger, spade, shovel, or garden trowel. When using a spade or shovel, take a thin slice from the side of a "V"-shaped hole. Place the samples in a clean bucket and mix them thoroughly.

Bring a minimum of 2 cups of soil per sample to your county Clemson Extension office or purchase a soil sampler mailer through Clemson University Soil Testing Laboratory (http://www.clemson.edu/agsrvlb/).

Included with the mailer are a soil sample bag and a "Soil Analysis" form. The Laboratory at Clemson analyzes the soil. The following pages include an example of a soil test report with accompanying recommendations and comments.

Agricultural Service Laboratory

171 Old Cherry Road, Clemson, SC 29634
http://www.clemson.edu/agsrvlb

DATE: 2/17/2006		LAB NUMBER:	6011816
SOIL REPORT FOR:		ACCOUNT:	0000000
		FARMER ID:	CHECK SOIL J
		SAMPLE:	1
CHECK SOIL J		SOIL CODE:	3
		CLU NUMBER:	
		BPH:	7.40

ANALYSES	RESULTS
Soil pH	4.3

			Very Low	Low	Medium	High	Very High
Phosphorus (P)	47	lbs/acre					
Potassium (K)	212	lbs/acre					
Calcium (Ca)	595	lbs/acre					
Magnesium (Mg)	119	lbs/acre					
Zinc (Zn)	1.8	lbs/acre					
Manganese(Mn)	152	lbs/acre					
Copper (Cu)	3.6	lbs/acre					
Boron (B)	0.1	lbs/acre					
Sodium (Na)	11	lbs/acre					
Sulfur		lbs/acre					
Soluble Salts		mmhos/cm					
Nitrate Nitrogen		ppm					
Organic Matter		% (LOI)					

LIME AND FERTILIZER RECOMMENDATIONS
Home Garden (Inorganic)

- Limestone: Apply 149 lbs/1000sq ft

- Test for zinc indicates there is sufficient zinc in the soil for good plant growth.

- Test for manganese indicates there is sufficient manganese in the soil for good plant growth.

- One pint (2 cups) of fertilizer is equal to approximately 1 pound.

- Per 1000 square feet (or 300 feet of row), apply 10 pounds of 10-10-10 before planting. At the same time add either 8 pounds of single superphosphate (0-20-0) or 3 pounds of triple superphosphate (0-48-0). Apply 10 pounds of calcium nitrate (15.5-0-0) or sodium nitrate (16-0-0) in a continuous band 4 inches from base of plants three weeks after appearance of first few leaves.

Home Garden (Organic)

- Limestone: Apply 15 lbs/100sq ft

- Test for zinc indicates there is sufficient zinc in the soil for good plant growth.

- Test for manganese indicates there is sufficient manganese in the soil for good plant growth.

- For optimum growth of garden plants, you should try to maintain at least a "HIGH" level of all the plant nutrients in the soil. This can be accomplished by additions of compost, manures, lawn clippings, etc. throughout the year. If any of the plant nutrients indicated on the soil test report fall into the medium or low category, the following materials may be added per 100 square feet to bring them back up to a high level. Phosphorus: 10 lbs of bone meal or rock phosphate. Potassium: 10 lbs of granite dust or green sand. Wood ash is high in potassium but should be used sparingly only on acid soils (pH less than 6.0) due to its potential to make the soil too alkaline. Magnesium: If limestone is recommended due to low pH, use dolomitic limestone which contains magnesium. If limestone is not recommended add 10 lbs of epsom salts. Calcium: If

Agricultural Service Laboratory

171 Old Cherry Road, Clemson, SC 29634
http://www.clemson.edu/agsrvlb

limestone is added as recommended due to low pH, this will correct low calcium levels. If limestone is not recommended add 10 lbs of gypsum. Nitrogen: If a nitrogen rich material such as compost or green manure (especially from legumes) has been incorporated in the garden soil within a few weeks before planting, little or no further nitrogen will be required. Otherwise, incorporate in the rows any one of the following materials soon before planting: 5 lbs of bloodmeal, 5 lbs of fish meal, 10 lbs of soybean seed meal, 10 lbs of cotton seed meal, or 15 to 25 lbs of poultry manure.

If you are a certified organic producer, be sure to check that the products you are using to meet the above recommendations are in compliance with the USDA National Organic Program Standards.

Strawberries

- Limestone: Apply 15 lbs/100sq ft

- Test for zinc indicates there is sufficient zinc in the soil for good plant growth.

- Test for manganese indicates there is sufficient manganese in the soil for good plant growth.

- Once a berry planting is established (1 year old for fall planted and 6 to 8 months old for spring planted areas), fertilizer needs are the same. However, in the early stages of growth the following procedures are suggested.

  For Fall Plantings:
  Two weeks before setting plants incorporate 1 pound of 10-10-10 per 100 square feet. When growth begins in the spring, broadcast ½ pound of 10-10-10 per 100 square feet; immediately after harvest apply 1 pound 10-10-10 per 100 square feet.

  For Spring Plantings:
  Broadcast and incorporate 2 pounds of 10-10-10 per 100 square feet about a week before planting.
  Fertilize again in mid-June and late September by broadcasting 1 pound of 10-10-10 per 100 square feet. Always apply fertilizer to the plants when the foliage is dry, and sweep the plants with a broom immediately following application.

  Second and Succeeding Years:
  After renovating, broadcast 1 ¾ pounds of 10-10-10 fertilizer per 100 square feet, and water it in. Fertilizer should be applied two more times during summer and fall. This should be done in mid-July and again in mid to late September by broadcasting 1 pound of 10-10-10 per 100 square feet. Just prior to the beginning of growth in late winter, apply ½ pound of 10-10-10- per 100 square feet. Continue this schedule for the life of the planting.

  If soil test Magnesium level is low and lime is recommended, use dolomitic limestone.

Annual Flowers or Roses

- Limestone: Apply 15 lbs/100sq ft

- Test for zinc indicates there is sufficient zinc in the soil for good plant growth.

- Test for manganese indicates there is sufficient manganese in the soil for good plant growth.

- As a precaution against fertilizer burn, water the plants immediately after the fertilizer is applied.

- Per 100 square feet, apply 2 cups 10-10-10 when spring growth begins and repeat monthly until August 1.

- Fertilizer should be spread uniformly over the area and soaked into the soil. If applied before planting, mix in the top 6 inches.

Agricultural Service Laboratory

171 Old Cherry Road, Clemson, SC 29634
http://www.clemson.edu/agsrvlb

SOIL TEST RESULTS

Your soil analysis will have a bar graph representing the amount of soil nutrients found and the soil pH value. It will tell you how much lime is needed to raise the pH to the appropriate value, and it will give you specific information regarding what type of fertilizer you need and how to apply it. These recommendations are specific for whatever type of plant you want to grow (as you indicated on the soil test record sheet when you submitted the sample).

UNDERSTANDING YOUR SOIL TEST REPORT

Soil pH: Soil pH is a measure of how acidic or alkaline your soil is. Soil pH directly affects nutrient availability. The pH scale ranges from 0 to 14, with 7 as neutral. Numbers less than 7 indicate acidity, while numbers greater than 7 indicate an alkaline soil. Plants thrive best in different soil pH ranges. Azaleas, rhododendrons, blueberries and conifers thrive best in acid soils (pH 5.0 to 5.5). Vegetables, grasses and most ornamentals do best in slightly acidic soils (pH 5.8 to 6.5). Soil pH values above or below these ranges may result in less vigorous growth or symptoms of nutrient deficiencies.

Nutrients: Nutrients for healthy plant growth are divided into three categories: primary, secondary and micronutrients. Nitrogen (N), phosphorus (P) and potassium (K) are primary nutrients, which are needed in fairly large quantities compared to the other nutrients. Calcium (Ca), magnesium (Mg) and sulfur (S) are secondary nutrients which are required by the plant in lesser quantities but are no less essential for good plant growth than the primary nutrients. Zinc (Zn) and manganese (Mn) are micronutrients which are required by plants in very small amounts. Most secondary and micronutrient deficiencies are easily corrected by keeping the soil at the optimum pH value.

Nitrogen: Available nitrogen is taken up by plant roots in the form of nitrate (NO_3-) and ammonium (NH_4+). Nitrogen testing is not recommended because the levels of available nitrogen are variable due to its mobility in the soil. The available forms of nitrogen are very water soluble and move rapidly through the soil profile with rainfall and irrigation. This causes the amount in the root zone to fluctuate over time. Recommendations are based on the requirements of the particular plants you are growing.